# Understanding People

# Books by Dr. Larry Crabb

# Understanding People

## Why We Long for Relationship

# DR. LARRY CRABB

**Z ZONDERVAN®**

ZONDERVAN

*Understanding People*

Copyright © 1987, 2013 by Lawrence J. Crabb, Jr.

This title is also available as a Zondervan ebook. Visit www.zondervan.com/ebooks.

This title is also available in a Zondervan audio edition. Visit www.zondervan.fm.

Requests for information should be addressed to:

Zondervan, 3900 Sparks Drive SE, Grand Rapids, Michigan 49546

This edition: ISBN 978-0-310-33607-5 (softcover)

Library of Congress Cataloging-in-Publication Data

Crabb, Lawrence J.,
    Understanding people.
    Bibliography: p.
    Includes index.
    ISBN 978-0-310-22600-0 (hardcover)
    1. Pastoral counseling. 2. Bible — Evidences, authority, etc. I. Title.
BV4012.2.C68   1987
    253.5                                                                87-14200

Cover design: Faceout Studio
Cover photography: gettyimages®
Interior illustration: gettyimages®
Interior design: Katherine Lloyd, The DESK

Printed in the United States of America

# Contents

# Preface

For some years now I have devoted considerable effort to thinking through the subject of biblical counseling. At least one conclusion seems clearly warranted: the ground to be covered includes an almost limitless assortment of thorny questions, each with the potential for creating division. And where the potential exists, the reality is not far behind.

Consider a few of the questions. First, *what does it mean to claim that a particular approach to counseling is biblical?* Certainly no evangelical would advertise that his or her ideas are unbiblical. Yet it seems that everyone who has taken a position on counseling has been criticized by someone else for being unbiblical. Christian counselors devote a good deal of their writing and lecturing to denouncing other Christian counselors as unbiblical in their views, or at least not as biblical as themselves.

Exactly how are we to measure whether a given counseling position qualifies to be called "biblical"? I recall one theologian suggesting that a training program in counseling would be biblical if it included a certain minimum of theology and English Bible courses. Behind his suggestion is the idea that counseling itself is "abiblical," a discipline quite separate from biblical/theological matters, but that surrounding counseling theory with enough seminary-level courses would lift it to the status of biblical. All of us within theologically conservative circles want to be biblical, but what is it that makes one approach biblical (or more biblical) and another unbiblical (or less biblical)?

Reflect on a second set of perplexing questions. *How are we to understand the relationship between biblical study and psychological inquiry?* Is a degree in theology irrelevant to becoming a good biblical counselor — or is it essential? Or simply helpful? Should Christians aspiring toward the ministry of biblical counseling study secular psychology? Will it corrupt their thinking or expand it? Is it better to examine secular theory under the teaching of secular professors, or should secular theory only be critiqued with the help of Christian professors committed to biblical authority? Or perhaps, if the Bible really is sufficient to answer every question about counseling, secular theory should be ignored altogether. Over the years, I have routinely received letters asking whether I would recommend enrolling in a secular or a Christian school to study counseling. What answer should I give?

Is a thorough grounding in Scripture sufficient to equip someone as an effective counselor? Or is further practical training required, both in the application of the Bible and the method of application? What credentials or training or experience would *you* look for in deciding where to send your anorexic daughter or your depressed father for help?

Third, *how should spiritual leaders in the church and trained counselors in their professional world work together to help people become emotionally whole and relationally effective?* Mark McMinn, professor of psychology at George Fox University, continues to argue for a collaborative relationship between counselors and the church, where the resources of wisdom and availability are pooled to best help the most people. Under Tim Clinton, the American Association of Christian Counselors equips licensed counselors to do their work either through the church or in professional settings. Less focus is given to encouraging church leaders to form entire congregations into healing communities. Is spiritual maturity by itself sufficient to qualify someone to help others with problems such as sexual addiction, eating disorders, borderline personalities, and panic attacks? Is that the naive position held by Christian idealists and properly panned by thoughtful realists?

How about Larry Crabb? Does he really believe what his more recent books suggest, that soul talk can connect people into a true spiritual community that takes the pressure off people and releases gospel power into their lives? Can well-meaning Christians be equipped to have conversations that matter, conversations that can better achieve what we wrongly assume can only happen in therapy?

Fourth, *what should we do with the tired but still live issue of self-esteem*? Must we love ourselves before we can love others? Or is self-love nothing more than sinful self-obsession? Look beneath all the current thinking in Christian circles about how people change and you will see lined up on one side of a deep valley a large group who warmly exhort us to love ourselves as a necessary precondition for loving others. "Love others as you love yourself" is their key text, interpreted to teach that "self-love" must be developed before "other-love" is possible.[1] The core problem behind surface troubles is understood to be low self-acceptance, which, in some people's minds, is really the essence of sin. Counseling efforts must therefore be directed toward helping people to accept themselves more completely.

There is another group who think that people are already too concerned with themselves and that efforts to build self-esteem aggravate the problem. The real problem is not unfulfilled longings, these folks claim, it is depravity. Sin has so blinded the hearts and minds of people that only truth from the Bible can bring the needed light. Study of God's Word therefore is a priority.

Counselors of this persuasion are regarded by self-love advocates as harshly insensitive to deep human needs, so caught up in their cold, stiff, exegetical position that they miss the warm truth of God's affirming love that throbs through the entire message of Scripture.

The Stiff Exegetes, huddled together across the valley from the Self-Lovers, suspect that self-worth is the enemy's Trojan horse, a ploy designed to bring within the walls of the city of God a godless humanism dressed up in Christian-sounding language. Their chief concern seems to be that a human-centered distortion of the gospel is hiding within any teaching that gives place to a concern for self-worth. Accordingly, they strongly disclaim and oppose such teaching, believing that they are contending earnestly for the once-delivered faith. They tend to regard self-love advocates as a mixed multitude — some sincere believers who want to be biblical, others holding to frankly liberal or at least neoorthodox theology, but all deceived, wrong, and potentially dangerous.

I find myself in clear alignment with neither group. The Self-Lovers seem to reduce sin to something less heinous than arrogant rebellion and foolish self-sufficiency, and they therefore propose a remedy too mild to deal with the real problem. Providing conditions for growth is inappropriate treatment when a fast-growing malignancy is the problem.

The Stiff Exegetes, on the other hand, unwittingly allow a proper concern for precise interpretation of the Bible to rob the text of its relational and life-changing vitality. In order to maintain a nonrelational, impersonal understanding of the Bible, they must neglect many passages that underline the importance of community and intimacy. Their approach often produces people who excel more in scholarship and theological rigidity than in love, nondefensive living, and chosen holiness. They would insist that proper exegesis of the Word never separates doctrine from practice, that the Word — understood, proclaimed, and obeyed — is itself sufficient to change lives. But somehow God becomes separated from his Word, and time spent in the Word doesn't quite get us to the Person who breathed the words we study.

The teaching of the Stiff Exegetes leaves large and significant areas of human experience untouched — and therefore unchanged.

*Vital truth* that penetrates to the core issues of life has somehow been replaced with *technical truth* that equips people to pass seminary exams and to preach exegetically correct sermons but not to communicate deeply, to relate meaningfully, or to proclaim truth to real human need. An understanding of Scripture that fails to answer the hard questions about how to involve ourselves productively in one another's lives is no real understanding at all.

All Christians who believe the Bible to be God's inerrant, authoritative, and sufficient Word earnestly desire that their thinking be governed by the text and that it enjoy clear biblical support. But as we go to the Bible in search of answers to the questions that regularly confront counselors (such as "What do I do with the withdrawn teenage girl who hates herself because her dad has been molesting her for three years and is still doing it?"), a fifth set of troublesome issues emerges.

*What principles of interpretation and application should control our efforts to draw from the text the information we need to help the victimized daughter?* Do we really believe that the Bible is the right book in which to find answers to these sorts of questions? If so, how do we guard against "finding" support for positions that we already hold *before* we come to the text? Is the sincere, regenerate counselor schooled in neither formal theology nor biblical languages capable only of eisegesis and therefore dependent on trained theologians for "real" exegesis? If so, why do biblical scholars rarely answer the hard questions people ask about living?

> An understanding of Scripture that fails to answer the hard questions about how to involve ourselves productively in one another's lives is no real understanding at all.

Is the Bible a textbook for counselors or is it not? Some insist that the Bible reveals everything we need to know to be thoroughly equipped for living as Christians but then (I think inconsistently) refer people with "psychological" problems to specialists with professional helping credentials (i.e., counselors with training in extrabiblical thought). They accept the commonly made distinction between psychological and spiritual problems and consult the Scriptures only when dealing with the latter. Is that legitimate? Do psychological disorders really constitute a category separate from spiritual concerns? If so, what defines the distinction? Maybe agoraphobia is nothing more than a label for something that, properly understood, will be recognizable as a spiritual problem that the Bible addresses, at least in principle. Perhaps psychological problems and spiritual problems grow from the same root.

If, however, there are two separate categories of difficulty, can we trust the unregenerate psychologist to enlighten us about psychological problems, just as we trust a competent physician, whether saint or sinner, to diagnose and treat medical diseases? Or was Cornelius Van Til correct in speaking about the noetic effects of sin that taint every conclusion drawn by a nonbeliever with moral error?

Perhaps we should return to the other possibility, that there is only one category of disorder, that so-called mental illnesses and neurotic reactions are really complicated spiritual problems, relabeled and disguised, but still matters for which the Scriptures provide an adequate framework for understanding. If we follow this line of thinking, what then are we to do with the mass of data painstakingly collected by secular researchers? Ignore it as useless? Select those parts of it that support biblical notions and talk of pagans stumbling onto truth? Reinterpret through a biblical presuppositional grid what has been observed by secular psychologists?

. . .

The questions are endless. So too are the various answers proposed by Christian responders. The situation in the field of Christian counseling resembles (in every bad respect) the splintering of the evangelical church into competing denominational camps, with each one protecting its unique distinctiveness with all the vigor of a fight for life, and with each treating the others with sometimes benevolent, sometimes contemptuous, disdain.

Denominations among Christian counselors include a diversity of more or less well-identified schools of thought, some with all the trappings of an established movement:

- Highly visible "name" leaders
- Ardent, vocal disciples
- Special conferences to which mainly the faithful come
- An approved list of authors and speakers
- Jargon that marks the user as among the initiated

The likelihood that substantial agreement will ever emerge from further dialogue and study is not good — no better, I suspect, than the prospects for developing an ecumenical position to which all conservative denominations would happily subscribe. Differences will remain, even among those committed to essential theological positions.

Perhaps this is not merely inevitable and therefore to be tolerated; perhaps it is good. In a world where the struggle to understand what God has said is carried on with imperfect minds, perhaps diversity of thought within a well-defined framework is healthy. Christians too often listen to one another in an effort to find points of difference rather than for mutual stimulation. The effect is to choke off the kind of creative thinking that could expand our understanding in uncertain areas.

Clearly articulating differing viewpoints and rambling about loosely formed ideas with a common commitment to let Scripture be the final arbiter could provoke productive examination of our own positions. We could then see more clearly where our understanding of things simply does not deal adequately with important issues. If we are in fact committed to a high view of Scripture, the effect will be to drive us back to the text, perhaps with new methods of study but certainly inflamed with urgent questions that need answers. In an atmosphere of mutual love, respect, and forbearance, dialogue could be profitable.

Dialogue among Christians (and non-Christians too), however, often degenerates quickly into division, tension, and hostility. A party spirit, nourished by misunderstanding and thoughtless rhetoric, encourages both a suspicious attitude toward any whose allegiance is outside our narrow circle and an unhealthy support for "our kind." Why? Why is the community of God's children so prone to petti-ness and clannishness and backbiting when we of all people should evidence the most compassion when we disagree with one another?

The answer, I think, is both simple and tragic: We are defensive, proud, and threatened people. Advocates of one position sometimes assume that their sole purpose in "inter-camp" contact is to inform and correct, never to listen. We convince ourselves that we are standing for truth when in fact we are unthinkingly defensive. Because we rarely examine our own motives as we dialogue, preferring rather to believe naively that the Spirit of God is prompting our fervor, the discussion ends with each side self-righ-teously committed to its own position and piously rejecting of any other.

> Christians too often listen to one another in an effort to find points of difference rather than for mutual stimulation.

There is such a thing, of course, as a legitimate stand for truth. Christian missionaries must enter a Muslim culture determined never to compromise the true gospel in their efforts to build bridges with the people. They *are* there to proselytize, to convert others from a false position to a true position. Their clear purpose does not include a synthesis of ideas through dialogue.

Christian counselors, too, believe that the truth of God is not a flexible set of loose concepts that happily accommodates any thought-through position. There is truth and there is error, and the Bible is the ultimate yardstick for measuring which is which. Among

Christians equally committed to biblical authority, there are sub-stantial disagreements over matters such as ecclesiology, eschatol-ogy, and pneumatology, and we should hold our studied positions with sincere conviction.

But within the family of those who confess the lordship of Christ and the authority of the Bible, certain attitudes should be character-istic. Outsiders should easily see that we speak with one another in a spirit of mutual support and love. Instead, I fear, they more com-monly observe an attitude that says, "I'll look to see where you step on my favorite toes, and then I'll pull back with a cry of righteous indignation."

When our views as Christian counselors differ (as they inevi-tably will), we must remain true to our convictions as we seek to make clear our distinctives. And wherever we believe there is out-right error or dangerous trends, we must take our stand, with gra-cious humility, but also with unwavering firmness.

The problem is that we really don't manage to do this very well. Our sinful tendency is rather to quietly and unself-consciously *enjoy* criticizing a position different from ours. We shake our heads in sad regret over our brother's or sister's error while our hearts beat with the happy excitement of felt superiority. Declaring where someone else is in error, especially to a like-minded audience of appreciative followers, can be a heady experience, something like leading a high school pep rally before the championship game.

As Christians we, above all people, should recognize how we can deceive ourselves by attributing noble motivation to pharisaical haughtiness. Knowing our bent toward self-exaltation, we must take special precaution as we express our differences with one another. We should spend much prayerful time in examining our motives, *expecting* to find self-serving purposes. We must avoid inflamma-tory rhetoric masquerading as bold denunciation of error, replacing it rather with passionate but reasoned discussion of a fellow believ-er's thinking. Boldness can easily become arrogance.

If the renewed (and welcome) concern with spiritual formation in evangelical circles is permitted to engage our continued interest in counseling that is biblical, we may see classical thought — Puritan soul care, Catholic mysticism, Reformed spirituality, desert wisdom — inform current dialogue about real change to shape a profoundly Christian understanding of personal growth. Hopeful glimpses of light are visible on the horizon.

But our efforts to understand and promote the kind of change made possible by Jesus still have the potential (some of it realized) to significantly divide rather than substantially bless. Our work can easily become a platform on which leaders erect monuments to themselves rather than serving as a framework for compassionate penetration of troubled lives with the truth of God. It can become the occasion for strife and hatred rather than the means of improving relationships among people who are commanded to love one another. But things could be different.

If biblical counseling is to realize its positive potential to glorify the God who alone can heal the brokenhearted and reconcile sinners to himself, I suggest that we submit ourselves to a few simple but easily violated guidelines as we discuss the subject.

*Knowing our bent toward self-exaltation, we must take special precaution as we express our differences with one another.*

**Guideline 1:** *Articulate our positions carefully and nondefensively.* Demonstrate their consistency with Scripture with a nonantagonistic fervor that matches our convictions about their validity and usefulness. Where conviction is tentative, fervor should be subdued. (Significant self-examination of our motives will be required to follow guideline 1).

**Guideline 2:** *Maintain a willing openness to changing positions we currently cherish if we come to believe that change is warranted by previously unseen insights into Scripture.*

Evidence such willingness by attending conferences taught by other evangelical counselors. Seriously study and consider their views through face-to-face dialogue. Invite theologians to evaluate our handling of Scripture.

**Guideline 3:** *Self-consciously labor to walk the tightrope of open conviction* by working to avoid falling into either (1) accommodationism (openness to the point where unity is placed above truth), or (2) exclusivism (conviction to the point where condemnation of another viewpoint precedes understanding it).

We should agree when we can, disagree when we must, and cooperate whenever possible without compromising the pursuit of godly purposes.

• • •

In this book I attempt to observe these guidelines. My purpose is to present some of the fruit of my efforts to understand biblical counseling. I do not intend to further the development of yet another counseling denomination. I do intend to offer my ideas in a fashion that will stimulate further discussion, clarify misunderstanding, and drive us deeply into God's Word with more questions.

Readers familiar with my earlier books will recognize movement in my concepts but not, I think, fundamental change. I continue to be quite comfortable with my earlier language. The human needs for security and significance are a shorthand way to express the deep longings in the human heart for relationship and impact. Either set of terms is fine with me. But some have interpreted me to teach that human needs for security and significance define our essential nature and therefore properly become our lifelong concern. The result, in the minds of some, has been a human-centered focus on fulfillment rather than a God-centered emphasis on obedience to God and preoccupation with his glory.

Because my choice of the term "need" has apparently communicated to a few what I do *not* believe and what I strongly oppose, I hope that referring to "deep longings that constitute the thirst that our Lord alone can quench" will better convey what I have always believed. Other movements in my thinking, some more than linguistic, will be apparent to the careful reader.

This book is intended to provide only a framework for thinking about counseling, discipleship, and spiritual formation. To know what questions to ask and what observations to point out during the counseling hour requires an intuitive feel for people that comes only through years of reflecting on people and working with them. Mastering the concepts in this book will not directly equip someone to function effectively as a counselor, but it will, I think, provide a basis for developing a good understanding of people. Discussion of how change occurs in people and how counselors promote that change must build on an understanding of how people operate and how their problems develop. This volume tries to lay that foundation.

As I write this book, my sincere prayer is that there will be a growing and friendly concern among evangelicals, splintered on many issues but united on essentials, to honor the preeminence of Christ and the authority of the Bible in all our counseling efforts.

# Jesus Is the Way

For I resolved to know nothing while I was with you
except Jesus Christ and him crucified.

**1 CORINTHIANS 2:2**

I sometimes wonder if the solutions to life's problems are perhaps much simpler than our psychologically sophisticated culture expects them to be. The intricacies of Freudian theory have become less intriguing to the average person in today's world than they used to be, and pop psychology, whether in Christianized or secular form, has retained its appeal now for decades. Many people are drawn to simple, uncomplicated answers to life's most profound and troubling questions.

Perhaps the trend toward simple answers is good. Too often, of course, it encourages people to swallow naive ideas that ignore real complexities that must be taken into account for an adequate understanding of things. The trend may also reflect a desire to find painless, quick answers to replace the need for walking the costly path to real happiness.

But still, an openness to believing that there are simple answers may be an advantage. Perhaps the answers to important questions really are simple. Solutions to puzzling personal problems may be difficult to put into practice, but perhaps they are easy to grasp, or at least to state.

During literally thousands of hours spent trying to keep couples together, it has occurred to me more than once that if husbands would more strongly involve themselves with their wives and if wives would quit trying to change their husbands, most marriages would really improve. There's nothing complicated about that. The major obstacle getting in the way of doing it is stubbornness, not limited understanding.

Children, I suspect, would become more manageable and infinitely more lovable if parents would answer, properly and with some consistency, a few elementary questions that all kids ask. First, "Am I loved?" Correct answer: "Yes, deeply — and here's the unmistakable evidence of my rich, committed involvement with you." Second, "Can I get my own way?" Correct answer: "No, not without cost — and here is a sample of the painful consequences that result from bucking against God's plan."

People with anxiety disorders (a fancy label for people who have more anxiety than most) might find more peace by checking out where they think God isn't quite up to handling their future and learning to take his promises more seriously than by swallowing pills and searching for the roots of their fears in childhood traumas.

Depression might lift more enduringly when people grasp the realities of the Christian purpose for life and hope for tomorrow than if they were to dump their repressed grudges and hurts in therapeutic catharsis.

"Trust and obey, for there's no other way to be happy in Jesus." Could it really be as simple as the hymn suggests? Why does this sort of thinking sound so hopelessly naive and dangerously superficial? Why do people who talk about "answers in Jesus" sound more like simple-minded fanatics than like reasonable professionals prescribing helpful solutions?

If there is a "simplicity in Christ" that applies to the field of counseling, it has consistently managed somehow to elude the grasp of most psychologists and theologians. Neither group has done an especially good job of getting down to a practical understanding of how humanity's fall into sin is related to anorexia, depression, homosexuality, and the like or how the solutions to these problems are to be found in Christ and Scripture.

Psychologists (and some theologians and preachers) often redefine sin as lack of self-esteem or inability to love — anything other than morally evil, blameworthy rebellion. With their backs turned to a radically biblical view of how sin infiltrates every fiber of human personality, they offer solutions to people's problems that do not require the atoning work of Christ on the cross. Their efforts to solve problems without Christ can be dressed up with such impressive theorizing and appeals to current research that God's ideas on solving the same problems seem helplessly general and hopelessly out of date.

Theologians (including and sometimes especially conservative ones) have been similarly disappointing in spelling out simple answers to life's pressing questions. With few exceptions, their technically competent and well-informed scholarship has produced more points to debate than principles to live by. Biblically documented truth has somehow been shorn of its relevance. Passionless orthodoxy has spawned a generation of rigid Christian leaders who simply cannot relate to people.

Please do not misunderstand me. I believe that foundational studies, which may have no immediate relevance to somebody's struggles, are legitimate and needed. The careful development of biblical and systematic theology must serve as the footing on which all else is built. And the tools of exegesis (biblical languages, contextual analysis, knowledge of culture) have real value.

> Passionless orthodoxy has spawned a generation of rigid Christian leaders who simply cannot relate to people.

But somehow a commendable commitment to exegetical precision has tended to yield thorough answers to many questions that disturb no one but fellow scholars. And worried parents, hurt spouses, stubborn depressives, and self-hating bulimics turn in vain to Bible teachers for answers to their urgent, personal questions.

Something is wrong. All true theology, in its very nature, is intensely practical. There is no legitimate separation between the academic, the devotional, and the practical study of Scripture. Each is inseparably related to the other. Divine truth is always intellectually acceptable, spiritually enriching, and practically relevant. If it is true, it has personal impact. Truth is always in motion, moving us toward deeper relationship. If motion is not apparent in our discussion, then truth is not understood.

But for some reason, theological breadth provides no guarantee of spiritual depth or relational competence. Exegetical skill built on a familiarity with the original languages and the cultural context does not ensure there being qualified ministers to respond to the crying needs of their people. There is a wrongful division between the academic and the practical.

When psychologists don't grapple with the sinful roots of emotional disorders and when theologians separate scholarship from relevance, people are left to live their lives in confusion, wondering if the questions that keep them awake at night really have answers. Finding no real help either in a psychology that fails to direct them toward Christ, or in sermons that showcase the preacher's knowledge more than they penetrate folks with God's truth, troubled people are tempted to settle for solutions that substitute excitement for supernatural reality and immediate relief for lasting movement. As a consequence, scores of people today are caught up in a superficial and distorted version of what it means to trust the Lord. On the one hand, emotional highs have replaced quiet trust, and frenzied fanaticism is preferred to disciplined perseverance. On the other, Christians have settled into a pattern of ritual that amounts to little more than complacency and external conformity.

Pastors and other Christian helpers are in the same bind as ordinary Christians. They find little help either in psychological ideas stained with humanistic thought or in ponderously irrelevant theology. As a result, they too sometimes accept simplistic and useless but biblical-sounding ideas in their efforts to help people. Exhortations to confess sin, repent of it, and obey God's blueprints (all good and right things to do) are fervently delivered to confused people who don't quite understand what sin needs to be confessed or how changing certain behaviors will really help. And the ones giving the exhortations aren't clear themselves about how it all works. (Some hide their confusion behind stronger calls to repentance.)

Jeremiah had nothing but scorn for the shallow religious leaders of his day who "dress the wound of my people as though it were not serious" (Jeremiah 6:14). Prescriptions that fail to get at the root of an undefined problem can do real damage. They offer the promise of peace and health to the terminally ill without ever healing the disease.

> Prescriptions that fail to get at the root of an undefined problem can do real damage.

When I argue for simple solutions, I in no way want to be identified with either those shallow healers who speak glibly of faith and love or with the simplistic counselors who do little more than exhort surface change. I want no association with that brand of Christian counseling that fails to take into account the complexity of human problems or the slow painfulness of personal growth. Nor do I desire to affirm my belief in the sufficiency of Scripture and then mishandle the Word. I want neither to "eisegetically allegorize" and come up with fanciful speculation nor to "exegetically trivialize" and carefully organize an assortment of lifeless details.

My burden in this book is to lay a foundation for accepting the simple (but rather radical) idea that Jesus Christ is the way, the truth, and the life without falling into shallowness or irrelevance. To reach that goal, it is necessary to see how psychological disorder is really the product of the sinful pursuit of life apart from God. It is further necessary that we develop an approach to Scripture that enables us not only to understand but also to be affected by its truth. Such an approach will, I believe, permit us to see the relevance of biblical truth to conceptualizing and treating emotional disorders.

Three assumptions govern my thinking as I reflect on the nature of biblical counseling:

1. If properly approached, the Bible is sufficient to provide a framework for thinking through every question a counselor needs to ask;
2. Relationship with Christ provides resources that are utterly indispensable in substantially resolving every psychological (i.e., nonorganically caused) problem;
3. The community of God's people functioning together in biblical relationship is the intended context for understanding and living out God's answers to life's problems.

The book is organized around these three central ideas. Part 1 deals with the sufficiency of Scripture for every counseling question. Part 2 develops a view of people and their problems that makes it clear why Christ is necessary to every counseling solution. Part 3 looks at the process of substantial change in the human personality and points out how biblical community can function as the ideal context for that sort of change.

# Part One

# A SUFFICIENT BIBLE
## Finding Answers in Scripture

## Chapter 1

# How Do We Know What To Believe?

I think you need more than biblical counseling," a pastor recently told a troubled young woman. "Your problem seems far too deep for what I can offer you. In my opinion, you need to see a professional counselor who can get all the way down to the buried emotional roots of your difficulties."

The pastor then referred his client to a licensed psychologist who practices primal therapy, a largely outdated approach to helping that claims to deal with deep issues through emotionally reexperiencing the forgotten traumas of childhood.

Another pastor referred a depressed husband, whose wife had rejected him, to a "rage-reduction" therapist. The pastor assumed from his limited knowledge of psychiatric theory that churning anger was beneath the man's depression and that counseling to reduce rage would therefore be helpful.

After several group sessions of rage-reduction treatment, the husband reported not only a new awareness of previously hidden anger but a new ability to openly (and sometimes crudely) express it to others. His depression lifted.

Another counselor offers her clients something she calls "re-parenting" therapy in which she frankly encourages them to become fully dependent on her as she assumes the role of a warm parent. The idea is that when people can relax in someone's love to the point where they feel comfortable with themselves and unthreatened by others, they will find the strength to meet life's challenges. Her appointment book is filled with hurting people who want to be re-parented.

How do we evaluate the dozens of approaches designed to help people solve their problems and live more effectively? There are family systems therapy, empirically validated eclectic therapy, rational-emotive therapy, cognitive-behavioral therapy, implosion procedures, dynamic psychotherapy, Adlerian counseling, nouthetic counseling, spiritual deliverance, love therapy, recovery groups, directive therapy, reality therapy — the list could continue.

**We must figure out a strategy for deciding what to believe.**

Both the secular and the Christian communities are overrun with ideas about growth and wholeness. Each claims validity as an explanation for how people function, why problems develop, and how change can occur. If we are to move about with any sense of clear direction in this raging sea of competing ideas, we must figure out a strategy for deciding what to believe. We want to know not only what will work, but as Christians we want to know what is true and right.

Our decision to accept a model of counseling should be based on more than the observed effects of the model. We must first concern ourselves with which ideas are true and which ones move people in directions that ultimately are good. Effectiveness is an important issue to be addressed, but only after we deal with accuracy and rightness. Yet how do we determine what is true, right, and effective?

. . .

Scientists work with different standards than the average person in deciding which ideas they will accept. In professional journals, psychologists must demonstrate research support for the ideas they advance. The more rigorous the research, the more credible the conclusions. In its effort to establish itself as a science, psychology has for more than half a century relied on an empirical approach to finding truth: just the facts — the observable, brute facts; if the data do not support the theory, throw out the theory.

But over the years, psychology — especially the applied areas of counseling and psychotherapy — has often granted a respectful hearing to experienced, able thinkers who have reflected on what they have seen in their consulting offices as their basis for developing coherent theoretical systems. Theories like those advanced by classical psychoanalysts such as Freud, Adler, and Jung, and more recently by psychologists such as Ellis, Perls, and Maslow, have little support in tightly designed research investigations, but they provide appealing explanations of human behavior and apparently useful directions for helping people. It is fair to say, therefore, that extensive experience with people coupled with insightful reasoning is regarded by many as a legitimate route to truth.

Occasionally a notion will seem to burst out of a creative mind without the support of either observed data or careful reflection, and people will uncritically swarm to it. Somehow the idea just "seems right." It fits. It feels good and it does something for people that apparently (and sometimes dramatically) helps. No one involved with the idea asks for proof; evidence seems quite unnecessary. People just give themselves to it because it seems right intuitively.

Christian counselors approach the matter of deciding what to believe very differently. Some depend on research support or clinical experience or tightly knit logic to defend their preferred hypotheses, but many appeal directly to the Scriptures to evaluate their ideas.

They claim validity for viewpoints if they are taught in the Bible, and they reject ideas that the Bible contradicts.

The Christian woman I mentioned earlier eventually questioned whether the practices of her primal therapist were biblical. "Is it right," she asked, "to go back to earlier pain and learn to fully re-experience it? Isn't that focus out of line with the biblical view of 'forgetting those things which are behind'?"

When the woman asked the therapist about her concerns, he responded without ever looking at the text his client was quoting to determine whether his treatment violated any of Paul's inspired teaching. His defense included a convincing appeal to (1) neurological studies on the brain's capacity to store repressed emotions; (2) the theory behind primal therapy, which teaches that undischarged earlier feelings can interfere with present, normal functioning; and (3) his experiences with scores of people unhelped by pastoral counseling who reported real improvement through his methods.

The rage-reduction therapist and the re-parenting counselor argued similarly for their theories but also mentioned as support several biblical concepts that were congruent with their ideas. "No, we can't prove the validity of all that we do by referring to specific passages in the Bible. But you must understand that the Bible was never intended to serve as a counseling textbook any more than it should function as a surgical manual for physicians. We must draw our ideas from psychological thinking and research but be careful to remain consistent with biblical teaching. We believe the Bible must be honored as God's Word."

Knowing what to believe about counseling is not simple. As we try to decide which ideas and methods we can embrace without compromising our Christian commitment, two central issues emerge that must be addressed.

The first is *biblical authority*. Christians who hold that the Bible is God's authoritative revelation of himself will refuse to accept anything that the Bible rejects. They want to live under the authority of Scripture. But doing so presents a few knotty complexities. For example, how can we be sure what the Bible affirms and what it denies? Godly counselors hold to opposing views on many theological matters that bear on counseling theory and practice. Perhaps the Bible doesn't even address questions that counselors must ask and that secular psychology has clearly addressed. Is there a legitimate place within a commitment to biblical authority for studying the findings of modern psychology? If so, how can we profit from research studies and theoretical presentations and still preserve what McQuilkin has aptly called "the functional authority of Scripture over the behavioral sciences"?[1]

The second issue that emerges as we work at deciding what to believe is *biblical sufficiency*. Is the Bible really sufficient to guide counselors as they face the bewildering variety of questions that counseling presents? Can they find help somewhere between Genesis and Revelation for dealing with an exhibitionist or an anorexic? Or was the Bible never designed to be sufficient for such questions? Perhaps we must recognize that the Bible's authority extends only to what it deals with and admit that it is sufficient to guide us in understanding spiritual matters like salvation and repentance and eternal hope, but that many immediate concerns of a counselor fall beyond its scope. Once we take that position, we may turn to other sources of help to think through areas the Scriptures never address without undermining the Bible's authority or denying its intended sufficiency.

> Counseling models must demonstrate more than mere consistency with Scripture; they must in fact emerge from it.

Suppose, however, that someone wants to argue (as I do) that biblical authority is a genuine concern because the Bible does provide a comprehensive framework for thinking through a counselor's questions. Then the burden falls on that person to define what biblical authority means and to demonstrate the sufficiency of biblical revelation. And that is my purpose in part 1 of this book.

In the remainder of this chapter and the next, I argue that revelation must be the basis upon which we develop and defend our counseling ideas. Chapter 3 assumes a dependence on revelation and takes the argument a step further by affirming our responsibility to evaluate every counseling theory in the light of Scripture. It is my view that counseling models must demonstrate more than mere consistency with Scripture; they must in fact emerge from it.

In chapter 4 we consider the confusing topic of biblical sufficiency. How on earth can we find biblical wisdom about paranoia and bulimia when no biblical author ever intended to write on those subjects? Must we violate every accepted principle of biblical interpretation to "discover" answers to a counselor's questions that simply aren't there? Or is there a legitimate approach to understanding Scripture that can provide us with a biblical understanding of every personal problem?

Let us deal first with the matter of the Bible's authority over the field of counseling.

## Four Ways of Knowing

In our effort to determine how we can evaluate counseling ideas, perhaps the place to begin is to survey how we come to hold opinions about anything. Four separate roads to knowledge have been identified by philosophers: intuition, reason, experience, and revelation. I will discuss each of these briefly (a thorough discussion would require several volumes) in an attempt to demonstrate that *without the framework and foundation of revelation, the other three paths to ideas will invariably lead us to concepts that are inadequate to guide a counselor.*

### Intuition

When people "just know" that a certain position is true, we say that they are depending on intuition. Some ideas slap us in the face with their obvious accuracy. No proof or reasoned support seems necessary to win our conviction that the idea is true. Intuition is the path to knowledge that requires only *subjective certainty* and not rational or external evidence in order to justify belief.

The roots of intuition are of course complex. John Calvin held that certain concepts are underived givens that all human beings believe as part of their God-given humanness. Others argue that intuition is nothing more than the product of years of experience and reflection that come together for a person in a moment of understanding. Regardless of its background, intuition is a process in which an idea emerges within one's mind with a certainty that seems to depend on undefined internal rather than external sources.

> Intuition is a process in which an idea emerges within one's mind with a certainty that seems to depend on undefined internal rather than external sources.

Counselors rely on intuition when they enter a session without a premeditated plan, hoping that the encounter with a counselee will generate a sense of which direction to go in. I suspect that a good deal of what passes for professional therapy (and a great deal of pastoral counseling) follows a theory so vague and general that much of what happens depends on intuition.

To depend so strongly on intuition is unnecessary. Let me explain why. If the subject about which we desire knowledge is something that follows no discernible pattern and is therefore completely unpredictable, then waiting for hunches to occur to us intuitively is the best we can do.

The subject matter for counselors, however, is a person. While there is much that is unknowable and therefore unpredictable about people, there *are* processes and principles that describe how people live. And we can figure out some of them. People don't just "happen." The urge to exhibit oneself or having panicky feelings in certain situations doesn't emerge spontaneously without a discernible history and cause. People choose and think and feel and crave in ways that can be at least partially understood and thoughtfully dealt with. We can therefore go beyond intuition (still allowing our hunches to play a part) in our efforts to work with people.

### Reason

The mind has been regarded by many as the center of the personality, the capacity that most clearly separates humans from animals. Aristotle held that our minds are capable of bridging the gap between the natural and the supernatural. Thomas Aquinas accepted the classical Roman Catholic idea that the fall of humanity into sin did not fully corrupt the mind. He held that our thinking ability remains largely uncorrupted and intact in spite of our sinfulness. It was from this premise that he argued for a natural theology, a way to God through human reason.

> People choose and think and feel and crave in ways that can be at least partially understood and thoughtfully dealt with.

As advances in knowledge continued, the mind was more and more valued as the supreme instrument for discovering whatever one wanted to know, whether about God, nature, or human beings. This worship of the mind led to something called rationalism, a belief that unaided reason is capable of understanding all that is true.

It is important that we distinguish between rationalism and a more modest use of reason. No one but an unthinking mystic is willing to accept an idea as true if it can be shown to be intrinsically unreasonable. And none but the same mystic seeks to understand what is true without depending on the clear functioning of the mind. Reason has an appropriate and vital place in forming our convictions.

But rationalists go further. They own no authority beyond their reason. Rather than simply trying to reasonably understand what may be going on, they require all data to fit within their framework of logic or they summarily reject them. They rebel against the view that every model of understanding people must have some very ragged edges.

Rationalism, when seriously followed, runs quickly into a major problem. When opposing viewpoints are defended as reasonable by two thinkers, what is to be done? It is silly to argue that my idea is true simply because I think it is when you think your competing idea is true. The only arbiter available to settle the matter is reason. But both of us claim that reason is on our side. Eventually, to prove my point, the best I can do is claim that my mind works better than yours and then hope that someday you will get smart enough to recognize the reasonableness of my ideas.

The mind, I suggest, is simply not up to the task of serving as final arbiter. People differ on what is reasonable. People sometimes resist rational argument for hidden reasons that "feel" sensible to them. Those who have tried to win an emotionally charged argument with pure reason as their only weapon can attest to its inadequacy. More is involved in forming ideas and convictions than logic.

### Experience

Another popular path to knowing insists that experience is the best teacher. Intuition is purely subjective; rationalism leads to irreconcilable differences of opinion. We need an authority outside our feelings and thoughts that can govern both. Empiricism is a philosophy of knowing that suggests that the hard data of observable and measurable experience provides the needed authority.

Whenever someone claims that an idea is true, the empiricist shouts, "Prove it! Where's the evidence?" For example, if a family counselor says that parents should spank their children for disobedience, the empiricist asks for data that demonstrate that spanked children turn out better, according to chosen and measurable standards, than unspanked children.

"It just seems like the right thing to do," says the intuitionist.

"Makes good sense to me," says the rationalist. "Stands to reason that if doing something gets you punished, you do it less."

"The Bible talks about using the rod of correction," argues a Christian.

Empiricists will be satisfied with none of these responses. Until they can point to a body of research that shows that spanking reliably produces desired results that nonspanking fails to produce, they will regard the issue as unresolved.

Most of us, it should be noted, operate regularly according to a careless sort of empiricism. Testimonies that claim that "I did it this way and it worked" convince us to give something a try. Politicians argue against a procedure that has been tried and failed. "Proven" methods of selling are proven according to their previous results.

I remember hearing of a respected Christian leader who responded to a question about the source of impact in his ministry. "I attribute whatever power I have to almost fifty years of spending at least one hour per day in prayer and Bible reading." The inference drawn by many was that an hour spent similarly in their lives each day would result in an increase in power. The argument is empirical; it persuades through an appeal to experience.

Empiricism has limits, however. First, the most empiricists can do is report data and generalize about patterns. They can only say what is, never what ought to be. Empiricism can never serve as the route to moral truth. Description is the legitimate province of the empiricists; prescription is out of their territory.

Second, empiricists can never say anything with certainty. The most that they can claim is a regularity in observed data that supports certain hypotheses about how things work (and such claims are valuable for the Christian to study). But no one has observed all data or all possible data. Although I have never seen a river divide to form a dry path through the center, I cannot say that it did not or that it could not happen. All I can say is that I (and many others) have never seen it happen. Empiricism can juggle probabilities, but it cannot establish certainty. Another way of saying this is that empiricism can serve as the pragmatic basis for action ("I think I'll look for a bridge to get across the river rather than praying for it to divide"), but it cannot determine the truthfulness of an ultimate proposition (such as "there is a God who can divide rivers whenever he takes a mind to").

Third, empiricism is confined to looking at what it can see. Observable data form the entire basis of empiricism, and that severely limits what empiricists can talk about. Many important realities are not easily reduced to what can be seen: love, meaning, joy, grief, justice, to name but a few. When empiricists decide to study this sort of reality, they must define them in terms of their observable evidence. But in so doing, they find that the very reality they describe slips through their fingers. Few of us are satisfied with measuring a man's love for his wife by how many times he kisses her or how often he offers an unsolicited compliment. Empiricists who undertake to study the intangible world usually end up investigating elements that don't really matter very much, except to journal editors.

. . .

Our efforts to decide what is true are rather frustrating so far. Should Christians undergo primal therapy to resolve deep conflicts? How do we answer such a question?

*Intuition* requires us to wait for subjective certainty to emerge. But people have been "sure" of error before. *Rationalism* encourages us to think it through or to rely on the opinions of better thinkers than ourselves. But the best thinkers think differently. *Empiricism* challenges us to look at the results: has primal therapy cured depression in the past? But the data are confusing. Every system of counseling claims impressive results. Moreover, every system is haunted by horror stories of damage it has caused. And even if there are results, are they good results in a moral sense? Empiricism can't tell us.

We need a means of knowing answers to important questions other than intuition, rationalism, and empiricism if we are to arrive at a position in which we can have confidence. And there is one more possibility, *revelation*.

In the next chapter we discuss revelation as the basis of knowledge and consider some of the problems that come when we seek to depend on revelation for answers to questions about counseling.

## Chapter 2

# The Bible Warrants
# Our Confidence

I f we accept revelation as a prerequisite for developing a model of counseling, particularly a model in which Christians can have confidence, we must take a hard look at exactly what that means. How has God revealed truth to us? Where has God revealed what counselors need to know in order to help their clients? How do we get a hold on that knowledge once we know where to look for it?

The very idea of revelation implies a revealer, someone who lets others know at least a little of what he knows. Christians believe that God exists, that he is a real person who thinks, chooses, and feels, and that he loves his creatures enough to tell us what our problems are and how we can solve them.

According to most theologians, God makes himself known today primarily by two means, nature and the Bible. The first is referred to as *general revelation,* a term describing the fact that we can learn important truths by observing the created order: such as, there must be a creator to account for creation; an orderly creation reflects the work of an orderly mind, so the creator must be intelligent; a world in which personality exists can only be explained by a personal creator; and so forth. Careful observers can also notice regularities in how things work and thereby "discover" more effective remedies for human illness and better ways to build bridges. Science owes its very existence to the predictability of cause-effect relationships observable in our world.

*Special revelation* is a theological term referring to that divine disclosure that goes beyond the world of nature to give us more specific details that we must know in order to live, but that we cannot discover through the scientific study of his general revelation. In the Bible, God has spoken from his mind to our minds using language, a medium of communication that is rationally apprehensible. Our task is to use our minds to understand and grasp what he has said and then to submit our wills to that message.

Whenever we are persuaded that the ideas we live by come from God, it is fair to say that we are claiming revelational dependence. Many people today, including songwriters, counselors, and cult leaders, claim that God has revealed certain things to them. The immediate problem is to determine when that claim is legitimate. Indeed, "hath God said" what we think he has said? When Christian psychologists support an opinion with psychological research, can they argue that God has revealed himself through the scientific investigation of God's world? Or would Christian counselors who offer their understanding of a biblical passage as authority for their ideas be on safer ground in asserting revelational dependence?

In the preceding chapter, I argued that intuition, reason, and experience lose their value when they operate without regard for revelation. When people discount revelation by rebelling against the fact that all search for truth represents an effort to know God and what he has done, then their search becomes a journey through a maze without a guide. Revelation built on the fact that God exists and that he speaks to us must be the premise and the context for all our thinking. Calvin makes this point:

As the elderly, or those with poor sight, can hardly make out the words in a book, but with the help of glasses can read clearly, so Scripture crystallises ideas about God which had been very confused, scatters the darkness and shows us the true God clearly.... We take the first step towards true knowledge when we reverently take hold of the testimony God has graciously given about himself. Not only does a true and complete faith originate in obedience, but all sound knowledge does the same.[1]

Christian psychologists and counselors would, I suppose, wholeheartedly agree with this sort of elementary beginning. But when people move from a stated "commitment to revelation" to actual efforts to develop a view of counseling, how they depend on revelation must be carefully examined. In my view, many Christian counselors have adopted a method of study that treats the Bible as helpful, informative, and insightful — but neither authoritative nor sufficient. As a result the Bible is weakened. No longer is Scripture permitted to speak with a final word. We rarely turn to its pages for answers to certain kinds of personal questions. Psychology has usurped the place of the Bible in the minds of many who would strongly argue for revelation as the necessary route to knowledge. Perhaps affirming a commitment to a revealing God and to his revelation in the Bible and nature is not enough. If we are to maintain any valid concept of biblical authority, we must consider how to approach the study of counseling.

One method of study that seriously undermines any meaningful notion of biblical authority might be labeled "the two-book view of revelation." Let me explain this viewpoint. God has written two "books," nature and the Bible. Students of revelation should study both books to understand better whatever field of knowledge concerns them, whether medicine, astronomy, political science, or psychology. If God has spoken more clearly in one place than another about a particular subject, then we should spend more time studying the more relevant book.

Christian dental students, for example, do well to bury themselves in scientific texts rather than in Paul's epistles when they want to understand gum disease. But when their questions have to do with defining sin and learning how to overcome it, reading the Bible is appropriate. The Bible reveals nothing about gum disease, and dental textbooks never attempt to define sin. The questions we ask, therefore, determine which book we should read.

Many Christian counselors take this approach in their efforts to figure out people and their problems. The collection of ideas derived from our direct observation of people we call "psychology." The organized product of biblical study is called "theology." These are regarded as complementary disciplines, each contributing important data to our theory of counseling.

The two-book view, and the approach to integrating psychology and theology that it suggests, can be sketched rather easily, as shown in figure 1.1.

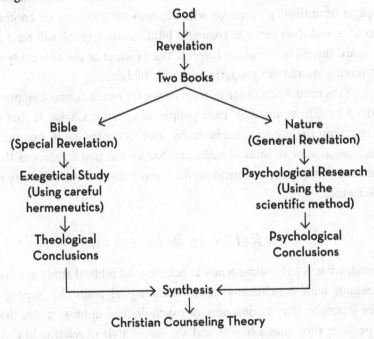

*Figure 1.1*

Most models of Christian counseling use this approach.[2] Often, when this line of thinking is followed, more time is spent in psychological reasoning and research than in Bible study, and for good reason: the Bible speaks only indirectly to many questions that counselors ask. The principle of investing time in the more directly relevant of the two books can lead to a neglected Bible. When Christian counselors are challenged to give the Bible more attention, the common response is to argue that the Scriptures were never intended by God to serve as a textbook for counselors. His "other book," we are told, is better suited for that purpose.

Notice where this reasoning leads. Our efforts to understand counseling do not need to be *guided by* the Bible; we must only make sure that whatever conclusions we reach are *consistent with* the Bible. The difference between "guided by" and "consistent with" is enormous. The theorist who is guided by the Bible more fully acknowledges its authority. Someone who depends for guidance on another source and then seeks to maintain biblical consistency will tend to regard the Bible merely as helpful. The product of the latter way of thinking should not properly be called "biblical."

This model is, as I see it, responsible for much counseling practiced by Christians that leads people away from Christ. If that is true, then the model must be faulty; and its central fault, I suggest, is a weak view of biblical authority. Notice the two features of this model that destroy any meaningful commitment to the authority of Scripture.

## A Return to Rationalism

First, what is to be done when conclusions of biblical study are discrepant with conclusions from psychological research? Suppose, for example, that a consensus of psychological opinion states that spanking promotes a hostile and aggressive style of relating in children. Suppose further that most exegetes conclude from Proverbs

22:15 that spanking is regarded by God as an effective disciplinary strategy for reducing hostility. What now? Do we follow psychology or theology? Or do we rearrange our understanding of one to make it fit the other? If so, which one do we rearrange? What should we tell parents to do when their children disobey?

Two-book theorists correctly point out that we can have total confidence in neither set of conclusions. Both psychological study and theological study require the use of finite and fallen minds. The ideas we come up with, whether from nature or the Bible, may misrepresent the truth God has revealed. No matter how strongly some may argue for an inerrant Bible, we cannot invest *our understanding* of the Bible with the same confidence that we place in the text itself. Similarly, the findings of scientific research may reflect our sometimes faulty perception of things rather than the real facts of nature.

When discrepancies occur between our theology and our psychology, we are encouraged by two-book thinkers to reevaluate both sets of conclusions. With this, I want to state clearly, *I agree.* That is exactly what we must do. Our understanding of either the text or the natural data may be faulty. But the attitude with which we reexamine the two books, in my view, must be carefully watched.

Two-book theorists argue that we must restudy both sets of conclusions — with no greater hope of finding "psychological truth" to which we can commit ourselves in the Bible than in the laboratory. Revelational dependence therefore leads us to an uncertainty from which neither the Bible nor science provides escape.

And what happens? Parents wait for a word from the Christian experts. But the experts have no sure word. In a consistent use of the two-book method, discrepancies between biblical and psychological conclusions can only be resolved through *personal judgment.* Revelation is in effect scrapped, and human reason becomes the final arbiter. The claim made by two-book theorists that they depend on revelation is invalidated by their inevitable return to rationalism and/or empiricism.

## All Truth Is God's Truth

A second feature of the two-book view that disturbs me centers on the use it makes of the truism that "all truth is God's truth." The truism is accurate. Truth is truth, whether scientific truth or theological truth, whether found in the psychologist's laboratory or in the Bible student's library. To speak of biblical truth as somehow more authoritative than scientific truth is really absurd. Truth has authority over error, not over another truth. One truth may enjoy greater *relevance* to a specific question than another truth, but no truth is more authoritative than another truth. The authority of truth lies in its truthfulness, not in the place where it is found.

> One truth may enjoy greater *relevance* to a specific question than another truth, but no truth is more authoritative than another truth.

If we continue the argument by asking which "book" has greater *relevance* to counseling, a fair case can be made for affirming that the Bible has more to say to counselors than the science of psychology. When counselors sort their way through the tangle of symptoms and complaints, they will eventually confront basic concerns about love, purpose, and sin. If the Bible is God's revelation about the essentials of what it means to live, then we should expect to find answers to the core questions within its pages.

But my concern for the moment is less with *relevance* than with *authority*. Since all truth is God's truth, is it reasonable to argue that truth from the Bible is somehow more authoritative than truth discovered in the lab?

As noted earlier, we cannot escape some degree of uncertainty when we declare our understanding of what is true, regardless of whether we appeal to Scripture or to science. In every attempt to define truth, we use our limited and corrupted minds. Because the effects of the Fall extend to our power of reasoning, we must admit that although all truth is God's truth, our understanding of what is true may not be true at all.

The flow of this logic moves us inevitably toward a hopeless skepticism in which we are destined to wander through life guessing which path we should take. Thus my two concerns with the two-book view. The first, as I have said, is that it forces us to retreat to rationalism whenever our theology contradicts our psychology. The Bible is no longer granted a meaningful role in final arbitration.

My second concern results from the first. It involves how we respond to the uncertainty intrinsic in all our formulations (an uncertainty that exists, by the way, even when theology and psychology appear to be mutually supportive). In the face of inescapable uncertainty, perhaps the most appealing criterion for choice is pragmatism: what works for me right now to produce what I value? If primal therapy brings relief from emotional tension, why not take advantage of it? The complaint that the theory of primal therapy may not be true loses force if we concede that no one can know what really is true. If re-parenting counseling helps an unhappy woman to feel secure, who can argue against it?

In a world where truth cannot be heard, results speak the loudest. The two-book view — some forms of which hold that because all interpretations are subject to error, we should depend on as broad a base of data as we can — moves us away from biblical dependence and toward rationalism and eventually empiricism. When discrepancies occur between the conclusions of theology and psychology, reason your way to an answer with no attitude of submission to biblical data. That's rationalism.

And because all our conclusions, even when they enjoy the support of both theology and psychology, must still remain tentative, our decision to act must be governed less by what we think is true (since we simply do not really know) and more by what we think will produce immediate, tangible results (at least those we can measure). That's empirical pragmatism.

## An Argument for Biblical Authority

If there is a way out of depending on rationalism and pragmatism as we try to figure out how we should counsel, it will only be found by demonstrating that our potentially errant conclusions from biblical study deserve greater weight in our theorizing than our potentially errant conclusions from scientific study. If somehow the Bible is to regain a position of real authority over science, it must be shown that it is reasonable to place more confidence in our biblically derived ideas than in hypotheses generated from our study of psychology. Both may contain error. But are we safer in relying on one more than the other?

Notice carefully what such a demonstration requires. We must argue that *less error* is likely to infect a counseling model built on biblical foundations than one developed according to scientific research. And that is precisely what I want to argue.[3] Four points form my argument.

1. God's *purpose* in revealing himself in the Bible is different from his purpose in revealing himself in nature. In nature, God unveils his "eternal power and divine nature" (Romans 1:20) in order to drive people to their knees in accountability to their Creator. Certainly it is proper to study the physical universe to understand better how things work so homes can be heated in winter and ear infections can be cleared up; but God's moral purpose in nature is to make himself known as someone with whom we must reckon.

In the Bible, however, God does much more. His moral purpose in giving the Scriptures is to graciously point out our plight, inform us of his solution to the problem, and instruct us how to accept that solution. In a word, the Bible tells us how to find life. And that is what counseling is concerned with: helping people who are experiencing problems that rob them of life to overcome those problems and live as they were designed to live.

Nature was not designed to be a textbook on life. The Bible was.

The problems people bring to a counselor always involve a malfunction in life: anxiety that keeps agoraphobics indoors; depression that takes the joy and meaning out of living; compulsions that drive people to do things that interfere with normal functioning—all obstacles to effective living. If counselors are supposed to help people live their lives as life was meant to be lived, and if the Bible is the book where God tells us how to solve our problems in order to live, then it follows that we should expect the Bible to provide more help to counselors than the scientific study of nature.

> Nature was not designed to be a textbook on life. The Bible was.

2. The *plainness* of the Bible is reason to turn to its pages with confidence. Although there is much that is hard to understand in Scripture, it still is revelation in propositional form; that is, it consists of ordinary words spoken by real people to other real people about rationally expressible matters. Nature is not propositional revelation. It illustrates rather than speaks; it presents us with unspoken observations that require translation into verbal symbols in order to be understood. A picture may be worth a thousand words, but when precision of meaning is what you're after, sentences do a better job. The superior clarity of propositional revelation over any other form is argument for depending more on the Bible than on science in developing a counseling model.

3. The *purity* of the Bible as uncorrupted revelation contrasts with the defectiveness of a groaning and cursed nature. Whatever the Bible says can be trusted, because the effects of sin have been supernaturally blocked from staining its teaching. But nature has not been so protected. What we learn from nature may reflect the results of sin. If scientific surveys report that couples who have enjoyed premarital sex experience greater emotional satisfaction in marriage than couples who were married as virgins, the data exist only because of sinful processes that distort life from the way it was meant to be.

We may, of course, learn lessons about industriousness from the ant, but only because the Bible authorizes the instruction. If we were to follow other examples in nature without worrying about biblical warrant, we might prey on the weak, sleep all winter, or copulate at will. Whatever the Bible tells us to do, we may do with confidence that we are on the right path because the Bible is perfectly moral in its teaching. Nature is not. Conclusions reached from biblical study, therefore, deserve more of our confidence than ideas we learn from natural study.

4. We have the explicit *promise* of the Holy Spirit's help when we come to the Bible in an attitude of teachable humility and personal honesty. Scientists have no such promise in their study.

Four reasons (and there are others) — the purpose of the Bible, its plainness, its purity, and the promise of the Spirit's help when we study it — combine to justify more confidence in the potentially errant conclusions reached through studying Scripture than in the potentially errant conclusions of scientific research.

. . .

As I seek to develop a model of counseling, I begin with the conviction that my study of God's written Word must be allowed to control my thinking more than any other data. Where the Bible speaks, it speaks with authority. Where it doesn't speak, we may look to other sources of information for help.

> Where the Bible speaks, it speaks with authority. Where it doesn't speak, we may look to other sources of information for help.

Studying the thinking of other people, whether Christian or not, can be legitimately provocative. The data and theories of psychology can serve as catalysts, stimulating us to consider new directions in our thinking. Both our power of reasoning and our intuition must be permitted a role in our efforts to build a counseling model. But in all that we do, the Bible must provide the *framework* within which we work and the *premises* from which we draw our conclusions.

The Bible does speak to much of what a counselor deals with. And (as I hope to show) it provides a basis for understanding *every essential issue* with which counselors struggle. To argue for biblical authority in the field of counseling means therefore (1) that we must come to the Bible in a spirit of expectancy and submission, and that (2) although we may regard the ideas of psychology as stimulating and catalytic, we may never regard them as authoritative. The actual data of psychology research cannot, of course, be disregarded. We must face whatever we observe and then come to the Scriptures for an understanding of why the data exist and what we should do in response to what we observe. But in every case, the instruction of Scripture must be final.

In this chapter I have affirmed not only that we must depend on revelation for our ideas about counseling, but also that biblical revelation must function as the controlling guide for all our thinking about counseling.

Now I want to advance the argument one step. It is one thing to assert that the Bible should be our authority in all that it addresses. It is quite another to hold that the Bible does in fact deal with all the questions that counselors ask. In the next chapter we move from considering the *authority* of the Bible in developing a counseling model to discussing its comprehensive *sufficiency* for that task. And that discussion requires that we take a look at the difficult subject of biblical interpretation: if the Bible is sufficient, how do we find answers in the text to the questions counselors ask?

## Chapter 3

# Does the Bible Speak Meaningfully to Every Human Problem?

Is the Bible a textbook for counseling — or isn't it? Does it provide authoritative help in thinking through the tough questions counselors are forced to ask when they involve themselves in the messy details of life — or doesn't it? Can counselors learn from studying Scripture how to help someone overcome depression, or must they turn to other sources? Are there answers to questions such as "How do I handle a counselee's resistance?" and "What really causes bulimia?" hidden somewhere between Genesis and Revelation? Or was the Bible never intended by God to provide answers to "psychological" questions?

Whatever questions the Bible answers, it answers accurately — perhaps not as thoroughly as we would sometimes like, but always correctly. When the Bible does answer a counselor's questions, we must accept the answers as authoritative. Whenever answers are not there, then it is necessary and legitimate to take our unanswered questions elsewhere.

I must make a vital distinction between two categories of problems, each generating its own list of questions: (1) problems resulting from physical/natural causes, and (2) problems resulting fundamentally from moral causes.

Under the first category, I include problems such as:

- Some (but by no means all) instances of depression and other affective disorders
- Behavioral or emotional problems stemming from chemical imbalance, physical lesions, or degenerative disease (e.g., menopause-related anxiety symptoms)
- Learning disabilities caused by perceptual malfunction, early learning deficits, or the like
- Drug-induced psychosis

Problems of the second kind are those that can be traced to a chosen strategy (although the fact of the choice may be denied) for handling life's struggles that conflict with a deep trust in the Lord and that do not reflect an increasingly thorough response of obedience.

As I hope to show in part 2 of this book, most of what presents itself to a counselor falls within the second category and therefore can be rightly responded to as essentially moral problems. In this chapter and the next, I want to argue for the intended sufficiency of the Bible to provide a clear and adequate structure for understanding and dealing with problems in the second category.

Let me state the question simply: *Is the Bible sufficient to provide a framework for answering every question that confronts a counselor?* Once the matter of biblical authority is settled, the issue of sufficiency must be considered. It does no good to affirm the Bible's authority and at the same time to deny its *intended* sufficiency. It therefore becomes critically important to determine which questions the Bible was meant to answer sufficiently.

At least three different positions may be taken.

1. No, the Bible is not sufficient, because it does not directly answer every question about how life should be lived on this earth and about how life can be lived according to an effective pattern.

2. Yes, the Bible is sufficient, because it does directly answer every question about how life should be lived on this earth and about how life can be lived according to an effective pattern.

3. Yes, the Bible is sufficient, because it provides either direct information or authoritative categories for answering all questions about how life should be lived on this earth and about how it can be lived according to an effective pattern. Whenever the Bible is not explicit about a given concern, biblical categories provide a framework for thinking through an adequate response to that concern.[1]

As we think through each of these positions, keep in mind that I am assuming the Bible's inspiration, inerrancy, and authority. Whatever the Bible says, it says correctly. Its teachings are binding. The point now is to examine the matter of sufficiency: does the Bible say enough to meaningfully guide Christian counselors in all that they do?

## Position 1

The Bible does not directly answer every legitimate counseling question. It is therefore necessary and right to turn to the data and theories of psychology for help.

Is the Bible a counseling textbook? "Of course not," say many Christians. "God never planned to write a comprehensive guide for counseling any more than he set out to instruct plumbers how to unclog a sink. The Bible deals with spiritual matters. Plumbers are concerned with sinks, dentists with teeth, and counselors with psychological problems. Let your area of concern determine which books you read."

If we follow this line of thinking, we may turn to the ideas generated by psychological research and clinical experience, not merely to be stimulated with observations that require explanation, but to find basic answers to important questions about life that the Bible simply does not provide. The Scriptures, many admit, spell out doctrinal and ethical positions that we must follow, but details of counseling understanding and method must be learned through other means. Content other than biblical data is permitted to serve as the beginning and end points for thinking through the issues of counseling.

Notice carefully how the word "biblical" is defined if we follow position 1. A counseling model may be called biblical if it never *violates* clear biblical teaching about doctrine or ethics. The concern is not whether our ideas about counseling *emerge* from Scripture, they simply must not *contradict* Scripture.

It is true, of course, that many Christian counselors who hold to a less than high view of the Bible are perfectly comfortable with such thinking. Let the Bible speak to religious concerns, but for answers to many important questions about living, give central place to the work of modern psychologists.

Yet it is also true that some conservative evangelicals who strongly teach the inerrancy and authority of Scripture really live by this first position. Consider what happens in many (certainly not all) Bible-preaching pulpits.

Preachers remain safely distant from troubling realities of their people's lives, shielded by their commitment to exegesis. "Husbands, love your wives," the pastor begins. And for the next thirty minutes the pastor's congregation listens to the results of careful and sincere study of the text.

During the exposition, a thirty-two-year-old insurance salesman glances uneasily at his wife, a woman who for some unknown reason provokes an incredible rage in him nearly every time she speaks. The sermon adds to his guilt. He approaches his pastor for help.

"I've tried to love my wife with the kind of love Paul speaks of in Ephesians. But I just don't know how to do it," he admits during his counseling appointment. "I've asked her to forgive me, I'm spending regular time in Bible reading, but it's just not working. For years now, I've tried to act lovingly, hoping the loving feelings would come. They haven't. What do I do? Just keep on as I have been doing?"

"Ryan," the pastor suggests, "God's power is available to you to really love her as you should. If you sincerely want to be God's man for this woman, then your job is to honor your commitment to the Lord and to her. Keep in mind that biblical love is not feeling, it's action. Keep on doing what you know is right."

A few weeks later, Ryan returns for another session. "Pastor, I've tried to do what you said, I really have. But it's getting worse. Last night I hit my wife for the first time. I hate myself for it, but I'm scared that I might really hurt her sometime."

At this point many godly pastors would feel terribly out of their depth. And rightly so — because they haven't had experience in dealing with violently angry people. Referral to a professionally trained counselor seems appropriate.

But why? Is there more to the referral than concern that Ryan receive the very best help? I suspect that beneath many referrals by *pastoral* counselors to *professional* counselors lies more than acknowledged inexperience. The issue that troubles me is that referrals sometimes reflect a pastor's belief that the Bible is really not sufficient to provide the needed help. Some obscure their real viewpoint when they suggest that people will be more open to the real answers of Scripture after the emotional roots of their problem are understood.

The point to notice is this: no real thought is given to the notion that perhaps the Bible can guide a counselor in dealing with Ryan's severe anger.

Most Christians lack confidence in the premise that the Bible speaks meaningfully to every issue of life. Seminaries unwittingly strengthen that quiet doubt when they fail to confront students thoroughly and specifically with the troubling questions about real living that people ask:

- How do I resist the urge to masturbate?
- I worry about money a lot. How do I stop?
- What do I do with the fear of living alone that I've felt ever since the rape?
- I just can't get close to people. How can I get over my social awkwardness?
- Why do I feel so empty? Where's the abundant life?
- How should I handle my husband? He worries so much about how our kids will turn out that he's always preaching to them.

Students who express concern for the practical relevance of their technical study may be reminded that God's Word has power and that the task of the preacher is faithfully to proclaim its message. The thought seems to be that the sort of problems mentioned will quietly disappear if people are caught up in the great truths of Scripture. Pastors therefore don't need to be concerned with the confusing and sometimes ugly details of people's lives. The purifying effect of biblical teaching will somehow clean out people's lives without pastors ever having to involve themselves in open, supportive, confrontive community.

The effect of such thinking is to deny fellowship some of its real value in preventing hardness (Hebrews 3:13) and provoking increased love (Hebrews 10:24). Our churches degenerate into audiences rather than communities. Nothing matters but the pulpit.

But honest pastors who are aware of what is happening in people's lives soon realize that personally significant questions are being asked for which they have no answers. And so they refer to trained counselors, being uncomfortable with their inability to bring Scripture to bear on certain areas of life, but consoled by the thought that those matters represent psychological rather than spiritual problems.

The view that good preaching and serious Bible study will solve personal problems without direct involvement with those problems provokes in me another concern. I sometimes wonder if the professors who teach this view most rigidly are not guilty of stubbornly looking away from such problems for their own protection. Perhaps some of them have no idea what to do with the tough questions people ask. Maybe their own lives are plagued with difficulties that remain unresolved. Rather than running to the Scripture with the urgent questions raised by real life, perhaps they retreat from people and their questions behind the acceptable barrier of scholarship. The tools of exegesis and the principles of hermeneutics can then become the means of denying the reality of unsolved problems. Real life remains unexamined and real-life questions remain unanswered while preachers proclaim a lifeless version of the living Word.

> Something is wrong when the message from a loving God to the people he created becomes more an academic treatise to be studied rather than wonderful truth to be grasped and breathed.

I address this matter carefully, for I do not want to be misunderstood. The careful and scholarly study of Scripture is vitally important. Knowledge of Hebrew, Aramaic, and Greek and an awareness of the cultural context of biblical literature is unarguably valuable. Developing principles of interpretation that prevent us from giving free rein to our imaginations as we interpret and apply the Bible is worthy labor — and students of the Bible do well to study these matters diligently.

But somehow the work of exegesis and interpretation as usually practiced has removed us too far from the realities of people's lives. Something is wrong when the message from a loving God to the people he created becomes more an academic treatise to be studied rather than wonderful truth to be grasped and breathed.

The concern to bridge the gap from what the text means to what it means to people today is not, of course, a new one. But I think it remains a real concern, and one that is largely unresolved.

Perhaps the crux of the problem lies less with the methods of Bible study and more with the *purpose* of our study. I wonder if the emphasis on scholarship in many of our seminaries represents in part a concern *not* to discern the real meaning of the text, but rather to avoid humbling contact with the confusion of people's lives. Perhaps it is easier to track down the etymology of a rarely used Hebrew word than to grapple with the present realities of stubborn problems in the living. The theological library becomes for many a hideout from life rather than a study from which we emerge equipped with God's living truth and prepared to move into the deep parts of people's lives.

The results are tragic. Churches led by pastors who fail to see the urgent relevance of the Bible to every aspect of life become mini-seminaries that continue the tradition of retreat and denial behind bold affirmation of orthodoxy. The message in such places is clear: *The community of God's people is no place to deal with the real concerns eating away at your lives; we exist to maintain orthodox belief and to promote conforming behavior. Helping you with your personal problems is not the business of the church.*

But why not? Why is it not the business of the church to lead people into an understanding of life that gets at the root of deep personal problems — problems that we all have?

The church should feel no guilt if it fails to sponsor a dental clinic or a classroom for learning disabled children. Those are legitimate concerns, but they do not represent the unique calling of the church.

The church has the responsibility to teach the message of the Bible and to promote patterns of life that reflect that message. If the Bible does *not* concern itself with emotional problems, then it is right for the church to refer those concerns to competent specialists who will not undermine biblical faith.

We must be clear on this. Whenever a Bible-believing church regards its mission as *not* including ministry to the deep personal struggles hidden in all of us, it is stating in effect that the Bible does not speak to those concerns.[2]

If, however, the Bible was intended by God to tell us how to understand and deal with the problems that interfere with life as it should be lived—if it really is a counseling textbook—then every nonorganic counseling question should be answered within the Christian community as it turns to the Bible for answers.

And here we encounter a basic hermeneutical problem. Perhaps the most highly regarded principle of biblical interpretation, at least in conservative circles, is "stick with the text." We are strongly cautioned to say neither more nor less than the original writers intended to say to their audience. When we abandon this principle in an effort to find "deeper" meaning in Scripture, our understanding of God's message is controlled, not by the inspired words of the text, but rather by our own imagination.

When we see in the text what (for whatever reason) we want to see, then our study fails to pull out of the Bible what is already there; it rather puts into the Bible what we think should be there. To avoid preaching a message with only the authority of human wisdom, preachers must be fully instructed by the text, proclaiming only what it says and the implications of its content.

As I understand it, this principle is the cornerstone of modern conservative scholarship. Evangelicals do, of course, insist that the Bible presents a unique problem for interpreters because the words of Scripture represent more than the expressions of mere mortals. They are God-breathed and therefore reflect not only the conscious purpose of their human authors, but also the intent of the eternal God. We are therefore permitted to find in the text a *relevance* that goes beyond what the human authors could have possibly anticipated.

But in our search for relevance, boundaries must remain in place if our efforts to relate the Scriptures to modern life are to be guided by more than human ingenuity. Somehow the applications to contemporary situations should be tied to the plain meaning of the text if they are to enjoy the weight of divine authority.

It seems to me that this responsibility to glean God's message from the text rather than from our fertile imagination is a difficult one to honor — necessary but still difficult. No one ever comes to the Bible as a high-quality blank disk ready to record faithfully without distortion whatever is heard. We all approach the text as persons with a history and with a present filled with bias, predispositions, and expectations. It is simply impossible to sort out fully and identify (let alone effectively resist) the host of influences that pull us to interpret a passage in one way or another.

These influences, I suspect, will vary according to the setting in which we function. It is one thing to work at sticking with the text when our job is teaching in a classroom or writing articles for theological journals. The expectations of the theological camp with which we are identified will, along with many other influences, tend to pull us toward certain interpretations.

It is quite another matter, however, to remain faithful to the text when God has placed us in the middle of hurting people who approach us every day with urgent questions about their lives that no particular passage seems to answer. What do we do then?

Sensitive pastors, who sincerely want to stick closely with the text *and* respond meaningfully to people, face a very real tension. They long to be relevant to the pressing concerns of people, but their commitment to say no more than the Scriptures say seems to block them from addressing those concerns directly.

At first glance, it seems that there are two ways to relieve the tension: either ignore the questions people ask, or stretch the Scriptures to cover their questions. The history of allegorical interpretation, in which figurative significance is attached to a text with little or no regard for its plain meaning, is filled with illustrations of forcing a passage to be relevant. God's handling of Elijah's depression after his run-in with Jezebel (he prescribed a long nap, among other things: 1 Kings 19) may be interpreted to mean that people should take a break when the ministry gets rough. Good counsel, perhaps, but it doesn't emerge from the text. Biblical content plus human imagination fired by a commendable concern for relevance does not yield authoritative principles by which to live.

The other option for relieving the tension between faithfulness to the text and relevance to life's questions brings us to position 2.

## Position 2

The Bible directly answers every legitimate question about life and is therefore a sufficient guide for counseling.

Many Christians insist that the text of Scripture, understood according to its plain, literal meaning, is comprehensively relevant to every *legitimate* question that life presents. The effect of this viewpoint is to disregard important questions by calling them illegitimate. Let me explain how this happens.

Paul's words to Timothy affirm that the Bible is able to give wisdom for finding life, that all Scripture is inspired and profitable, and that it provides everything we need to be fully equipped for living life as God intended (2 Timothy 3:15–17). It follows, some say, that if the Bible does not answer a question about life, the question does not need to be asked.

But what about "psychological" questions, such as what causes agoraphobia or how should we help someone overcome a poor self-image? The thinking of many is that psychological problems, when examined closely, will be recognized as nothing more than the fruit of unbiblical living. Therefore the cure is to *teach* people how to live, *rebuke* them for living wrongly, *correct* them when they go astray, and *train* them in godly patterns of living. And the Bible (in the 2 Timothy passage) claims to be profitable for exactly those tasks.

The problem with this reasoning, in my view, is that it is so close to being right. I believe in the sufficiency of Scripture. I believe that psychological disorder, when unmasked, will be seen to reflect spiritual disorder. However, when we raise our voices in favor of a radical commitment to biblical sufficiency, there is danger of losing depth in our understanding.

> When we raise our voices in favor of a radical commitment to biblical sufficiency, there is danger of losing depth in our understanding.

Two things in particular concern me, and they concern me enough to reject position 2 as stated.

My first reservation is that *it is possible to give to the literal meaning of the text a comprehensive relevance that it simply does not have.* Let me illustrate.

A man with strong urges to dress in women's clothes decides, after wrestling with embarrassment and shame, to confide in his pastor in looking for help to understand and resist these compelling desires.

The pastor turns immediately to Deuteronomy 22:5: "A woman must not wear men's clothing, nor a man wear women's clothing, for the Lord your God detests anyone who does this." The pastor explains that even though this teaching is embedded in Old Testament law, it reflects essential truth about an unchanging distinction between male and female and is therefore binding today.

Thus the matter is settled: it is sinful to yield to those perverted urges. God has spoken. The man either obeys or stands in rebellion.

And the man agrees. He knows it is wrong to cross-dress, but the urge seems overwhelming at times and he asks for help in obeying God's prohibitions. Again, the pastor responds with a verse: "The temptations in your life are no different from what others experience. And God is faithful. He will not allow the temptation to be more than you can stand. When you are tempted, he will show you a way out so that you can endure" (1 Corinthians 10:13, NLT).

Again, the counselee agrees. But again, he has more questions. In some cases, of course, continued questioning may reflect an effort to sidestep his responsibility to obey clear biblical instruction. But in other cases the questions may be sincere. Perhaps the counselee really wants to know why he feels those urges when most other men don't; maybe he suspects that those desires are related to other sinful patterns that, if dealt with, might reduce the intensity of his urges to a more manageable level.

But if we follow the thinking of position 2, these questions are illegitimate and should not be asked because no passage literally exegeted directly responds to them.

I grant that questions concerning the reasons for transvestite desires do not need to be answered before obedience to God's orders becomes a moral obligation. But perhaps a clear understanding of transvestism would open the door to repenting of subtle sinfulness energizing those desires. As he understood more of what was involved in his problem, maybe the cross-dresser would learn to rejoice more in God's grace and enablement. The chains of sexual slavery are strong. Breaking them may require more than holy determination.

Questions that go beyond the morality of transvestite behavior may, I submit, be legitimate — even though not directly answered in the text.

One more illustration: A woman panics at the mere thought of sexual activity with her loving, patient, and considerate husband. She asks why? The question, by the standards of position 2, is thrown out as illegitimate. Nowhere does the Bible clearly deal with that question, so it must not be raised.

The woman's counselor encourages her to ask another question, one that a specific text does address: "Is it morally right to deprive my husband of sexual relations?" Because there is a passage that bears directly on that question (1 Corinthians 7:5), the counselor confidently declares that sexual abstinence is permissible only by mutual consent for a brief time and only for the purposes of enhancing a couple's prayer life. Fear of intimacy is not an authorized reason for refusing sex.

The troubled woman, I suspect, would leave that counseling session utterly unhelped, and worse, significantly harmed. The sword of the Scripture was used less like a surgeon's healing scalpel than like an assassin's dagger. Under the banner of biblical sufficiency, Christian counselors may ignore crucially important questions by responding only to questions that they can easily answer. The result is a wider gap between the Bible and people's lives.

My second reservation about position 2 follows closely on the heels of the first. *When the range of permissible questions is narrowed, our understanding of complicated problems tends to become simplistic.* A commitment to biblical sufficiency has sometimes resulted in shallow explanations of complex disorders. And shallow explanations promote the unchallenged acceptance of superficial solutions.

Consider the problem of anorexia. I can recall how absolutely puzzled I was when I dealt with my first anorexic client: a pretty, sixteen-year-old girl who was thirty pounds below her normal weight—and she told me she was fat. How do you explain such a clearly wrong perception of oneself? To make matters worse, she was eating only a small meal every other day and was exercising madly in a determined effort to lose even more weight.

I once asked a man committed to the ideas reflected in position 2 how he would explain such bizarre behavior. It is difficult to come up with a biblical answer to a question that the Bible never seems to consider. My friend therefore changed the question from the one I (as well as the girl's parents) was asking to one that, in his mind, we *should* have been asking. The task as he saw it was to find a text where God had answered the questions that ought to be asked.

Two passages in the Bible (1 Corinthians 3:16–17 and 2 Corinthians 6:16) tell us that we are the temple of God; one passage indicates that our bodies are themselves temples of the Holy Spirit (1 Corinthians 6:19). My friend turned to these verses and explained that anorexia can be understood as rebellion against our responsibility to care properly for the Spirit's temple. This so-called biblical counseling will focus on developing in the anorexic a respect for her body and on exhorting her to treat her body accordingly. At best, the results of such counseling will be external conformity. The counselee will not be freed by truth to enter more deeply into loving relationship with God or with others.

When we limit the questions we are allowed to ask to those that the Bible specifically answers, the result will often be a nonthinking and simplistic understanding of life and its problems that fails to drive us to increased dependency in the Lord.

## Conclusion

The problem with both position 1 and position 2 is the same. Neither is able to draw truth from the Bible that adequately answers a counselor's necessary questions.

Position 1 doesn't even try, because it denies that the Bible provides all the answers a counselor needs to know. We must therefore look elsewhere for help.

Position 2 states that whatever information counselors need to know is clearly and directly taught in the Bible. Therefore only those questions that are answered directly in a passage are regarded as legitimate and necessary for a counselor to ask. The result is a shallow understanding of problems and solutions that sounds biblical but helps very few.

There must be another strategy for handling Scripture if the idea of biblical sufficiency is accurate. Because the Bible claims to be the word of life, we should be able to find within its pages all that is needed to counsel effectively. And we must find that information without stretching the text to allow interpretations that simply aren't there.

But how? How can we approach our Bibles to discern answers to the questions counselors ask? The next chapter describes a way to find within the intended limits of the biblical text all that a counselor needs to know.

Chapter 4

# The Bible Is a Sufficient Guide
# for Relational Living

Is the Bible a counseling textbook? The answer we give will depend on how we define counseling.

In the minds of many, there is a difference between *counseling* and *psychotherapy*. Counseling, some would say, deals exclusively with here-and-now concerns, attempting to help people cope with their lives more effectively by offering warm support and wise advice. Interpersonal skills like empathy, genuineness, and the ability to clarify, coupled with sensitivity and common sense, are the necessary tools.

Psychotherapy is very different, many say. It probes beneath present concerns (such as indecision regarding vocational choice) to expose an unconscious network of defenses, anxiety, and unacceptable or painful feelings that together generate the visible problem. Therapy deals with deeper issues than counseling because it looks beneath current complaints to the internal dynamics that really constitute the disorder needing correction.

That is the usual distinction: therapy deals with internal dynamics, counseling does not.

Freud is rightly credited with introducing the whole idea of *psychodynamics* to the modern mind. The term refers to psychological forces within the personality (usually unconscious) that have the power to cause behavioral and emotional disturbance. He taught us to regard problems as *symptoms* of underlying *dynamic processes* in the psyche. If his thinking on this point is correct, then counseling that tries merely to alter symptoms (for example, helping someone decide which vocation to pursue) is sometimes helpful, but always superficial. At its worst, it is no better than a physician prescribing aspirin for a headache when the cause of the headache is an operable brain tumor.

The influence of this element of Freudian theory in Western culture runs broad and deep. Perhaps the most significant effect is reflected in the degree to which we have bought into a "professional" model for understanding and handling personal problems. When Freud, a physician of some repute, made us aware of unconscious forces in the personality that can cause problems, people began thinking of them as *disease* processes and psychological *illnesses.*

The idea caught on: visible disturbances in people's behavior and emotions reflect invisible disorder in the dynamic structure of their personality. Counselors may effect some helpful change in the surface problems, but therapists trained in the science of psychodynamics are necessary if deep change is to occur.

Although there have been many challenges to dynamic theories of personality, most of the alternatives still hold to the essential idea of the professional model, that some sort of technical knowledge available only through professional training is needed in order to do "real" therapy.

According to this way of thinking, *counselors* — helpers whose training may not include the study of psychodynamics — are qualified to deal only with problems that are under the counselee's conscious, willful control. But when more help is needed, when wise advice, moral persuasion, and supportive empathy prove inadequate to solve the problem, then a professional *therapist* who knows how to identify and resolve deeper, more subtle concerns must be called in.

The point to notice is this: It is generally believed that a professional therapist is necessary to deal adequately with people at a deep psychological level. In a culture that accepts that premise, counselors are permitted a very limited role, parallel perhaps to the function of the pastor in a hospital. Both counselors and pastors must wait outside the door while therapists and surgeons enter the operating theater to cut skillfully and deeply into the roots of the patient's problem. Counselors support and pastors pray, but only therapists and surgeons heal. That is the professional model.

I think Freud was correct on at least three counts. He was right when he told us that we should look beneath surface problems to hidden internal causes. The Bible describes our hearts as deceitful, so much so that we regularly are not aware of our own motives (Jeremiah 17:9). Our Lord reserved his most stinging rebuke for people who dealt scrupulously with visible, external concerns while refusing to take a hard look inside where the real problems lay (Matthew 23:23–28).

> Counselors support and pastors pray, but only therapists and surgeons heal. That is the professional model.

Freud also insisted (I think properly) that in order to deal effectively and thoroughly with people, one must have a rather clear understanding of how human nature functions on the inside, where it is not possible to observe directly (Proverbs 20:5). Third, Freud was right in thinking that one necessary means of understanding other people's dynamics is first to understand your own (Matthew 7:3–5). It is for this reason that in most training programs every student who wants to do psychoanalysis must first be analyzed.

If the error of Freud and other dynamic theorists is *not* an insistence that we pay close attention to unconscious forces within personality, then what is it? I think a case can be made for asserting that their fundamental error is a refusal to study and accept a biblical view of human beings.[1] Because they have not accepted the guidelines of biblical data, their theorizing led them into an incomplete, unbalanced, and in some areas utterly immoral understanding of who we are as human beings and how we function. Had they submitted to the authority of Scripture as regenerate students of human personality, I believe their interest in psychodynamics would have carried us much further in our understanding than we are today.

The effect of that error has been profound. Not only has it led to a science of psychodynamics that denies important revealed truth about human nature, but it has also further discredited the Bible as a legitimate guide for understanding the deeper parts of the human personality. We can count almost on the fingers of one hand the number of thinkers who believe both that an understanding of dynamic functioning is important *and* that the Bible is an adequate guide for the task.

When we want to figure out why someone is a compulsive handwasher, the Bible is the last book we would think to open. Exactly what passage do we study to understand compulsive disorders? When we work with a homosexual, our Bibles tell us to regard homosexual behavior as sin and to exhort moral purity; but to understand why a man or woman is homosexual and what, if anything, can or should be done to change their sexual orientation, we read books written by professionals, not the writings of Moses or Paul.

I am convinced that we must challenge and overthrow this assumption of biblical insufficiency that the professional model has strengthened. I accept a distinction between counseling and therapy,[2] but I insist that the Bible is both essential and sufficient, not only for "counseling" in general, but also for that specific form of counseling that is commonly labeled "therapy."

In my view, the Bible teaches categories of understanding that can comprehensively guide our efforts to counsel with warmth and insight, *and* it lays out truths about human personality that are sufficient for leading us into a thorough understanding of what therapists call "dynamics."

When I argue for biblical sufficiency, I am suggesting that every question a counselor *or therapist* needs to ask is answered by both the content of Scripture and its implications. People who are struggling — whether they "go for counseling" or "enter therapy" — are having problems with living effectively as relational beings. Whether the problem began years ago with a rejecting parent or revolves around a current crisis with a rebellious child, the difficulty is finally with relationships.

The helper who seeks to intervene according to biblical wisdom will always work to improve relationships by helping people to change from the inside out. That is the end point, the final cure, the bottom line, the *sine qua non*: Relationship, first with God, then with others. And the Bible is a sufficient guide. It is a textbook for relational living.

We can now state the third response to the issue, "Is the Bible sufficient to answer a counselor's questions?"

Remember, position 1 said, "No, the Bible is not sufficient. Let psychology help." Position 2 answered, "Yes, the Bible is sufficient. But limit your questions to ones that are dealt with in specific chapter and verse."

Position 3, the viewpoint I hold and the one I want to develop in this chapter, may be stated as follows:

> Yes, the Bible is sufficient to answer every question about life, but not because it directly responds to every legitimate question. The idea of biblical sufficiency for counseling rests on the assumption that biblical data provide categories of understanding that have implications that comprehensively deal with every relational issue of life.

This statement may be awkward, but it permits us to honor the sufficiency of Scripture without becoming either simplistic or irrelevant. The statement can be graphically depicted as a model for finding biblical answers to a counselor's questions (fig. 4.1).

**A Model for Finding Biblical Answers
to a Counselor's Questions**

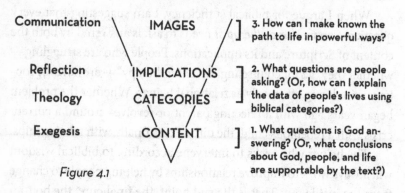

Figure 4.1

## Content: *Exegeting the Text*

Every responsible effort to develop a biblical understanding of counseling rests entirely on the data of Scripture. The message of God as made known in the Bible is the necessary foundation for building a model of biblical counseling. These are good words to conservative evangelicals, but they pose a few problems.

When a counselor with eight appointments the next day opens her Bible for an evening of study, she may experience significant frustration as she pores over her commentaries, Bible dictionaries, concordances, and lexicons. "Tomorrow I will counsel with a borderline personality, two depressives, one anorexic, the parents of a teenage drug abuser, a fetishist, and two married couples ready to break up. I just don't see how spending time in the Book of Exodus studying the garments of Israel's high priest or in the sixth chapter of Hebrews trying to figure out what the 'falling away' passage means is going to help me answer the questions those people ask."

The temptation is to skip the hard work of apparently irrelevant Bible study and move into more practical matters. And to do so, at least for the counselor, the Bible will be closed while she thinks through her approach to treating borderline personality disorder.

After all, where is a passage that discusses what a counselor should do with this sort of problem? Obviously there is none!

How then can we justify a counselor's spending a significant amount of time in serious Bible study? What does it have to do with her work? Certainly for her own spiritual growth, regular devotions and church attendance are appropriate, and for the maturing Christian a closer study of Scripture is essential. But where is the relevance of that study to her responsibilities as a counselor?

The relevance, I think, is very real. Perhaps it can best be understood by considering two separate kinds of questions: (1) the questions God has chosen to answer specifically in the biblical text, and (2) the questions we want answered as we struggle with our lives and the lives of others. It seems reasonable to suppose that these two classes of questions are not entirely unrelated. If God is at all interested in our struggles, then we may assume that the questions he bothers to answer are relevant to the questions we would ask if we had the sense to ask the right questions.

The fact is that our fall into sin has so warped our view of life that the questions for which we urgently seek answers may not be so important after all; or if they are good ones, they will usually be spoiled to at least some degree by our lack of wisdom.

Listen to the questions we ask:

- "How can I find fulfillment in life?"
- "How am I supposed to raise my kids so they will turn out right?"
- "Why can't I relax around people?"

These questions, and countless others like them, are clearly important to us and, in that sense at least, are quite legitimate.

But on closer inspection it will be seen that our questions often grow out of a demand that life work as we want it to along with a quiet unwillingness to look deeply and honestly at some ugly problems and internal pain hidden deeply within us.

Before we can hope to find wisdom for dealing with our questions, we must settle a few ground rules for approaching life's problems. And these ground rules are laid down in the answers God clearly gives in Scripture — things like who God is and what he expects, who we are as human beings and how sin has infected us, and how relationship with God and others is possible. Now the study of Aaron's clothing in Exodus 28 and the difficult passage on "falling away" in Hebrews 6 becomes relevant. Together with the rest of Scripture, they reveal truth about how God operates that must serve as the framework for thinking through our problems.

The first priority, then, in developing a biblical model of counseling is easily stated: study the content of Scripture. If this priority is set aside, we will develop counseling ideas and methods with appealing relevance to the questions people ask, but they will have no legitimate claim to biblical support. In many instances, because our uncorrected ideas about life are consistently wrong, the counseling approach we come up with will distort God's truth.

So exegesis of Scripture is our starting point. Every biblical counselor is responsible for spending time trying to understand the Bible. There are scholars, of course, learned in the biblical languages and aware of the culture of Bible times who can do exegesis that is more technically precise than that of Christian laypeople who lack this knowledge. It is wise, therefore, for people like me who have not had formal theological training to draw freely from the insights of the biblical scholars.

---

We often study the *Word* of God and miss the *message* of God.

---

There is a problem, however, with much that passes for exegesis, and biblical counselors must take this into account. When exegesis is seen as an end in itself — that is, when the conclusions of technical exegetical study are presented as the Word of God with little understanding of how these conclusions are supposed to influence people for God — then exegesis becomes a barrier to helpful involvement with people. We often study the *Word* of God and miss the *message* of God.

Knowledge — even that derived from good exegesis — puffs up. But love — a concern for entering into people's lives with the truth of God — edifies. Exegesis is the starting point, not the end.

Yet it is a necessary starting point. The principle is this: *Ask the questions that God has answered in the Bible in order to develop a framework for thinking through the questions that arise out of our lives.* Content study is the place to begin.

## Categories of Understanding

Simply stating what a given passage means does not exhaust all that is involved in Bible study. The next step is to organize the teaching of separate texts into broad statements of truth, or doctrine. Theology represents the effort to develop a coherent understanding of topics that the biblical data address.[3]

The usual chapter headings in systematic theology textbooks are the kinds of doctrinal categories I have in mind. Topics like anthropology (what does it mean to be human?), hamartiology (what is sin?), pneumatology (who is the Holy Spirit and how does he work?), and eschatology (what is God's plan for the future?) require theologians to define statements of positions that the text supports.

When theologians arrive at a position — on how men and women can be saved, for example — by studying the relevant passages in Scripture, they express their understanding in a doctrinal statement. Doctrinal statements, because they usually represent an effort to tie together a variety of passages, might well be called "categories of truth," or, more useful to counselors, "categories of understanding."

An unfortunate tendency in evangelical circles is to evaluate candidates' fitness for ministry solely on the basis of their doctrinal understanding and commitments. If they are orthodox in their beliefs, they are granted the stamp of approval by ordination. Not enough thought is given to the future pastors' ability to enter wisely and deeply into people's lives with the truth they believe.

All of us know the kind of seminary graduates who, after a year or two in the ministry, complain, "No one is asking the questions I can answer. I'm prepared to defend my views on baptism and the millennial kingdom, but people are asking me how to cope with alcoholic husbands or obsessive thoughts about harming their children. I'm lost. I think they should have hired a psychologist rather than a pastor."

The point is that if these pastors had thought through their doctrines from a relational perspective, they would feel better equipped to handle the problems they are facing. If the Bible really is sufficient to address a counselor's concerns, then there should be no need for psychologists, just better prepared pastors.

We simply must not assume that our work is finished when we have determined our doctrinal stance on all the traditionally important theological issues. That sort of knowledge is a necessary foundation, but it is not the building. Once we have come to some understanding of the questions that God answers in the Bible (derived from exegesis and theology), we are ready to use that understanding to think through the second set of questions, those that people ask as they struggle with life.

No seminary professor, of course, would deny the importance of applying the Scripture to life. Students are instructed in their homiletics courses to apply the text to where people live. Why, then, are so few seminary graduates prepared by their theological education to handle what confronts them in the real world, both in their own lives and in the lives of others? Why do pulpits often become a protection from facing people rather than a springboard for diving into their lives? Why do Bible teachers sometimes flaunt their knowledge of Scripture to avoid people, rather than use their knowledge of Scripture to help people?

The answer, I think, involves the degree to which most of us hold our lives together through denial. Christian communities somehow sense an obligation to maintain an image that things are really quite all right. We learn to cooperate in a conspiracy of pretense, to keep our lives polished on the outside,[4] and to deny both the emptiness and bitterness and discontent on the inside as well as our relational ineffectiveness and lack of real intimacy with others.

As a result we never become aware of some of the more subtle but terribly real struggles that life presents. We face the obviously painful realities of losing a job or the death of a child, but we rarely pay much attention to the "dynamic" struggles within, such as resentment toward a father who never showed involvement, a hunger for approval that began years ago with a critical mother, a sense of inadequacy rooted in a history of social rejection, a fear of men that can be traced to the experience of incest, a confused concern over whether to confront a withdrawn wife or to patiently love her, or a disturbing sense of contentment with surface relationships that neither offend nor deeply encourage anyone.

Too few people in positions of church leadership are willing to face these sorts of realities honestly. As a church we have lost touch with the questions that people would ask if someone gave them the opportunity.

Until we have the courage to drop our guard and honestly face the tensions, lusts, resentments, and fears that are eating away at us inside, we will never understand the extent to which the Scriptures apply to life. Until then, our feeble attempts to tack an application to the end of our expository sermons reach no one deeply; worse, they are harmful because they tell people who are hurting that the church has no answers, that for help with "those kinds of problems" they must go to a professional.

Our church and seminary communities have too often become polite societies with strict rules of etiquette designed to maintain our denial of who we really are and what problems we are facing. The result is a stiff, cold orthodoxy that squeezes the very life out of Scripture.

Only the "words" of God can be understood in a seminary

library or a scholar's study. To grasp the "message" of God we must take our understanding of the text and move deeply into the lives of ourselves and others, admitting confusion, praying for wisdom, sticking rigidly with only the essentials of our faith, and thinking openly about everything else.

If our "categories of truth" are to be recognized as "categories of life," if the truth of God is to be seen as the pathway to knowing God, then we must face the reality beneath the surface of our lives. We must intensely puzzle over why we've gotten into such an awful mess and what we can do to get out of it. The questions that a brutal realism about our lives forces us to ask must be brought to the Scripture with the confidence that there are answers.

- Why am I uncomfortable when meeting new people?
- Why am I jealous of the success of others, especially those in my field?
- What do I do with the terrible pain I feel whenever I remember my mother's suicide?
- How do I cope with the awful fact that my father was too weak ever to love me, to be there for me?
- What am I supposed to do with my deep desire to be a woman because I'm so scared of being a man?
- How do I handle my terrible fear that if I ever expressed how I really feel, no one would really want me?
- Why do I feel so threatened when someone successfully proves that I've been wrong about something?
- Why do I not want to admit my internal struggles?

These questions, we must realize, are not being asked only by patients in a psychiatrist's office. They are rumbling within the hearts of the worship leader, the small group leader, and the young couple who just started coming to church. All Christians have deeply troubling questions that should be asked. Many never voice them, however, because to ask them breaks the rules of our community.

Christians are supposed to have it all together. Many others have coped with life by denying their struggles for so long that they are really unaware they exist.

The Scriptures will never come fully alive until we bring all of who we are to its truth. Seminaries would do well, I believe, to divide their curriculum into two parts: one dealing with the questions God has answered in the Bible, and the second con-

> The Scriptures will never come fully alive until we bring all of who we are to its truth.

fronting our knowledge of the Bible with the questions people ask when they honestly admit their struggles with life.

If the seminaries were to do that, our doctrine statements would more clearly emerge as life-changing truths, as categories for thinking through all that is going on inside people, with the power to change people from the inside out. Until that happens, we are doing little more than preaching the gospel and instructing converts in an orthodoxy that requires them to *pretend* that they have been transformed.

## Implications: Thinking Things Through

As we expose ourselves to the confusing realities of human existence, we will be challenged to explain what we see in the light of biblical categories. Not only will we come to see biblical truth as the path to life, we will also grow in our awareness of how the implications of those categories can substantially explain what happens in life.

I remember when I first learned that most exhibitionists feel sexual relief, not when they expose themselves, but rather when they see their victims express shock. That is information. I learned it from talking to people and reading case histories; I did not learn it from the Bible.

Now, if I believe that biblical categories are sufficient for answering the questions a counselor will ask, then I must take that information to the Scriptures and think. I must first decide which biblical categories might be expected to have implications that will shed light on the data. Certainly the operation of sin is involved; I therefore will reflect on the theological category of hamartiology. What is self-deception? What is the purpose of sin? Why is it attractive?

I might also think through what brings pleasure to people by pondering the psalmist's statement that he longed for God the way a thirsty deer desires water (Psalm 42:1). Could legitimate longings for God somehow be perverted into a craving for bizarre forms of sexual relief? Perhaps the biblical category of male/female has implications that will help to put the puzzle together.

Perhaps the male exhibitionist desires impact, the sort of impact that God intended men to experience as they take hold of their worlds. Maybe he has come to the wrong and sinful conclusion that meaningful impact is not available to him and therefore feels a profoundly frustrating emptiness. Shocking a woman by displaying the physical evidence of his maleness may be his sinful strategy for finding the satisfaction he thinks he can find nowhere else. Perhaps the exhibitionist is an example of Jeremiah's description of thirsty people who hew for themselves broken cisterns, which hold no water but at least provide a temporary, counterfeit thrill of fulfilled maleness (Jeremiah 2:13).

The task of the Bible student is to think about life within the categories that the Scriptures provide. If we can demonstrate that our conclusions reflect reasonable implications of biblical categories, then we can rightfully claim that our ideas are biblical. The authority for our thinking depends on the degree to which it *necessarily emerges from clearly taught biblical categories.*

One of my personal ambitions is to think through every common human problem in light of biblical categories, to arrive at an understanding of what causes the problem and what can be done to grow through it toward spiritual maturity, toward the end for which God saved us. I believe that biblical understanding of problems that the Bible does not directly address is possible if we think through the implications of biblical categories for the data we observe.

In part 2 of this book I discuss my view of two central biblical categories — anthropology (who humans are) and hamartiology (what their problem is) — in a way that provides a framework for beginning the task of thinking through life's problems.

To understand the problems a counselor faces in a way that deserves the label "biblical," we must start with biblical categories derived from the text, gather observations from an honest look at life, think prayerfully until it begins to make sense, and then go through the entire process again and again. Expressed in a simple equation, the process looks like this:

Biblical Categories × Life's Observations × Reflection = Biblical Understanding

## Images: Communicating Powerfully to People

Biblical counselors want to understand people according to concepts (or categories) that are taught in Scripture. But they want to do more. Their ultimate purpose is to communicate what they know in a way that will change lives. The wise and talented surgeon who never operates does the world little good.

In this brief section I want to deal with the center of effective communication. Counseling techniques such as rapport-building, timing of interpretation, and advice-giving are important, but they are not my concern at

> The message we teach will normally penetrate others no more deeply than it has penetrated us.

this point. I want to emphasize a biblical principle that, if violated, will undermine the effectiveness of the most skillful counselor.

The principle is this: *The message we teach will normally penetrate others no more deeply than it has penetrated us.* This principle emerges from passages such as 2 Thessalonians 3:7, 9, where Paul invites others to follow his example.

For you yourselves know how you ought to follow our example, because we did not act in an undisciplined manner among you, … in order to offer ourselves as a model for you, so that you would follow our example. (NASB)

See also Philippians 3:13 – 17 and 1 Corinthians 9:4 – 27.

The Christian message especially is one that must take root in the very core of our being before we can proclaim it with power to others. Skill and knowledge without maturity in the things of Christ do not qualify someone to be an effective communicator of Christian truth.

Unless counselors face the reality of how sin is subtly operating in their own personality and have learned something of what it means to repent deeply, they will have little power in communicating what their counselees need to hear.

Good exegesis and careful theology enable us to *recite God's truth to others* accurately. Insightful reflection about the implications of those truths to real-life questions makes it possible to *present truth with relevance*. But only living the truth with growing consistency, always eager to better understand what it means to live in the freedom of grace, equips us to *communicate with power*.

It has long been recognized by students of literature that metaphor, analogy, narrative, and myth are effective vehicles for getting an idea deeply into the minds of people. When we form a *picture* of truth, it adds dimension to its mere statement and the point is more clearly made.

The task of counselors (or parents or preachers) is to embody in their own lives the truth they want others to hear. Then the sentences that describe the truth will be accompanied by powerful illustrations of the truth.

When people want to know what God the Father is like, we direct their attention to God the Son. Why? He is the "express image" (KJV) or "exact representation" of God (Hebrews 1:3). When our counselees want to understand how the truths of Scripture can deepen their relationships with God and with others and how improved relationships will solve the problems of life, we must be able to invite them to look at how we function as an image of what "lived truth" looks like and how it helps. Without an increasing understanding of how the biblical message works in our own lives, no amount of training in counseling theory or technique will ever produce a biblical counselor.

We must study the Bible, define our doctrinal positions, think through the implications of our categories of understanding as we honestly confront life, and seek to develop in our own lives the reality of power and joy that we claim is available in Christ.

Content, categories, implications, and images — these four elements combine to give us an approach to Scripture that demonstrates its sufficiency to equip us for the work of counseling.

The next step in equipping ourselves for that work is to define the human dilemma using the approach to Scripture we have just developed. This is the focus of part 2.

# Part Two

# UNDERSTANDING PEOPLE
## A Tarnished Image
## and Broken Relationships

## Chapter 5

# How Can People Truly Change?

P eople have problems. By the standards of a flabby Christianity
that is more concerned with how people look than with deep
relationships with others, things aren't too bad. Every congregation has its share of depressed people, unfaithful spouses, and rebellious students, but most of the saints are getting along quite nicely.

But when the measuring stick of panting after God with passionate love and serving others from compassion-filled hearts is applied,
more of us can be seen to fall short. Relationships, by that standard,
really aren't terribly good. It's not just the people struggling with anxiety attacks and misguided sexual urges who need help; it's all of us.

If we are to know how to move ourselves and others toward life
as it is meant to be lived, we must address three vital questions: Who
are we? Why do we have so many problems? What are the solutions?

We need to develop a model for understanding people, problems, and solutions that is broad enough to apply to situations generally and practical enough to apply to situations specifically. Part 2

discusses who we are and why we have problems. Part 3 will deal with solutions.

First, people. When we strip away the differences, what makes us similar? What do we have in common that defines us as human beings? In what ways is an African tribal chief similar to a North American grandmother? What do graduates of Harvard have in common with high school dropouts?

By what principles do people make decisions? What drives us? Where do emotions come from? Are there such things as unconscious motives and thoughts, or are those ideas nothing more than the clever and profitable figment of psychologists' imaginations? We need to know who we are and how we operate.

Second, problems. It requires little insight to conclude that something is wrong with people. The human machine has got its wires crossed somewhere. Some people get depressed when a friend is unkind to them; others seem happily oblivious to massive rejection.

Many of us wage an unsuccessful war against our urge to eat more than we should. A few exhibit commendable self-discipline. For increasing numbers of younger women, appropriate self-control changes into a determined pursuit of thinness through obsessive dieting, sometimes to the point of poor health and even death.

Most marriages begin with the warm glow of anticipated intimacy. Nearly one-half of them end in divorce. Most fall short of expectation. Sexual frustrations often remain unresolved and are handled by emotional and physical retreat. Strong sexual urges sometimes press so urgently for gratification that people sacrifice family and career for a few moments of corrupt pleasure.

Churches that begin with enthusiastic pledges of unity sometimes divide into two camps, resulting either in cold war, hot war, or a split. Some churches enjoy a measure of real unity, but none make it through without significant problems.

When we hear of a friend's child who gets in trouble, we may notice a smug satisfaction mingled with our sincere concern. At other times or with other friends, we sense a more thorough ability to weep with those who hurt.

What is wrong with us? We're really not very good at relationships. Why not? What is the root of our problems? That's the second question.

Third, solutions. The temptation to rush quickly to the end of the mystery novel must be resisted. The detective's clever conclusions cannot be fully appreciated without first understanding the complexities of the tangle he or she unravels. The same principle applies here: *an adequate appreciation of solutions depends on an adequate understanding of people and their problems.* The solution of Calvary, for example, is only valued to the degree that the problem of sin is grasped.

If we skip the hard and sometimes tedious work of figuring out who we are and why we struggle so much, then our efforts to help will be shallow and, in the long run, unhelpful.

One obstacle we encounter is that most of us lack a clear theory of change. How do hot-tempered parents develop patience with their irritating children? How do scared newlyweds become confident, loving partners? How does a Christian man or woman with a same-sex attraction learn to live authentically as a heterosexual? Most of us, including counselors and pastors, don't really know.

We know that people *should* change, that Christians *should* grow in Christ, and we believe they can. But beyond a few basic ideas about obedience, prayer, and time in the Word, we're not very clear about how change occurs or what prompts it. Too often we conceal our ignorance behind impressive discussions about theology or methods of Christian education or church structure. But what seems to be consistently missing in most of these discussions is a coherent, thought-through model of change.

At your next church board meeting, ask the members to state their views of how people change and encourage them to use personal illustrations of changes that have taken place in their own lives in the past year. Pin them down on exactly what was responsible for the change. It is very likely that you will hear a lot of tired clichés about the power of God and his Word that upon inspection are found to say very little. We really don't have a clear idea about the solutions to people's problems that we can translate into specific strategies for helping people.

> Our failure to articulate a model of change is directly related to our confused and shallow understanding of people and their problems.

In my view, our failure to articulate a model of change is directly related to our confused and shallow understanding of people and their problems. We're not going to do a very good job of helping someone overcome depression without understanding why the depression exists in the first place. We must have some clear idea of what is going on inside people before we can develop confidence in the directions we suggest.

Counselors too often avoid the confusion provoked by honest inquiry and cling comfortably to an appealing theory that at least seems to answer a few questions. It is tempting to ignore a few facts that might upset our hard-won conclusions and, like Dr. Watson, congratulate ourselves on a theory that is later disproved. The better route is the more painful one taken by Sherlock Holmes, who is willing to remain confused until every fact, even the most trivial, can be explained.

People, problems, and solutions: we need a model, a way of thinking through these matters that is flexible enough to handle all the data and concrete enough to guide us as we cope with life. As I survey the territory to be crossed, at least five observations seem important to me:

1. There are many different approaches to understanding people;
2. Each of us holds to some ideas on the subject, with varying degrees of precision and awareness;

3. Whichever view we accept will profoundly influence how we deal with people and with all of life;
4. Not all the approaches can be right. Many of the ideas contradict one another. Some must therefore be wrong;
5. If a personal Creator is behind all of life, then a true understanding of people, problems, and solutions must be possible.

One author has suggested that there are well over two hundred different models for understanding people in today's psychological marketplace.[1] With so many options to choose from, any attempt to simplify and categorize what is available will necessarily sacrifice comprehensiveness.

But perhaps the advantages of sorting through the confusion are worth the cost. If we can arrange the many approaches according to a few common themes, then we might have a better basis for evaluating the options and working our way through to our own conclusions. And, to repeat the concept developed in part 1 of this book, our yardstick for measuring the validity of any idea about people, problems, or solutions must be the content of Scripture.

## Three Basic Models

When a counselee tells us he or she is depressed, our first task as counselors is to assess whether the cause of the problem is physical. It is not germane here to discuss how to discern the criteria used to make that determination, so let us assume for the moment that we have correctly decided that there is no medical basis for depression. Now what?

In response to questions about possible links between the depression and life events, the counselee indicates that there is no clear trigger for the depression: no loved ones have recently died; health is good; family relationships seem intact; no major crises have occurred; job and income are providing reasonable satisfaction.

So often in working with people, no obvious direction presents itself as the path to follow. And even when a route does seem clearly indicated, it often leads to more confusion. Because people are confusing, counselors will inevitably follow directions suggested less by data from the counselee than by the theories they already hold.

In working with the depressed client, counselors will operate according to whatever understanding they hold of how people function, why problems develop, and what solutions are available. Looking at it in the broadest terms, we as counselors are going to be guided by one of three basic models. That is, most of the several hundred approaches to understanding people can be grouped under three categories: the Dynamic Model, the Moral Model, or the Relational Model.

According to the *Dynamic Model,* people are controlled by internal processes (often called personality dynamics) of which they are usually unaware. The roots of these dynamic realities and the source of their current strength are found in the past, in the person's childhood. Psychoanalysts speak of "genetic reconstruction," a term describing their efforts to understand how the events of childhood produced the feelings and attitudes of today.

Perhaps an unloving and domineering mother withheld needed affection from the developing child, and a weak, frustrated father failed to step in and take hold of his unhappy family. Dynamic theorists might wonder if the child developed (1) a disposition to both hate and fear strong-appearing women, and (2) an image of himself (patterned after his father) of a weak person who can handle his world only through compliance and retreat.

These dynamic processes (hate/fear for certain kinds of women and a poor self-image) represent the damage done in childhood that lies behind present problems and therefore needs repair. When disappointments occur in the life of this person, he responds according to the dictates of these unconscious dispositions, perhaps retreating from relationships with women but still counting on someone strong to come along and make everything better.

In the minds of many counselors using the Dynamic Model, this set of internal psychological processes is regarded as a sickness in need of treatment. The client is seen primarily as a victim of bad parenting, someone who is in need of extensive therapy aimed at uncovering and rearranging the personality structure. Whenever the client seems unable to change his style of relating in the present, it is assumed that he has not yet been freed from internal compulsions. More insight is needed; hence, continued therapy.

Because the Dynamic Model looks at problems as symptoms of an underlying illness, it has also been called a "medical" model of understanding people. Just as medical doctors treat patients for physical illness, so counselors offer treatment to patients suffering from psychological illness. The treatment consists essentially of a search for the hidden roots of the problem. Dynamic counselors assume that exposure of the roots leads to increased freedom in dealing with the present problem.

The *Moral Model* takes a view of people that strongly contradicts the Dynamic Model. Counselors with this view are concerned that any shift of attention away from problem behaviors may provide people with excuses for irresponsibility: "I can't help it if I'm too depressed to cut the lawn. I've got deep problems inside of me that haven't been cured."

To the Moral Model counselor, people are more stubborn than confused. The core of everything we do is not an alleged network of dynamic processes; rather, it is our willfulness. More than anything else, people are responsible for what they do. Good counseling, therefore, keeps the focus on chosen patterns of behavior. Improvement is measured in terms of changed behavior and is promoted by identifying irresponsible behaviors and exhorting appropriate change. Much of the content of Moral Model counseling involves stripping away the many excuses for continued irresponsibility.

Homework assignments play a significant role in Moral Model counseling. Instructions to spend regular time in Bible study and prayer or to compliment one's spouse or to balance the checkbook are regarded as central tools in helping people solve their problems. Whether by design or not (it varies), little attention is given to the motives beneath behavior other than to insist that right motives reflect themselves in right behavior.

The *Relational Model* takes issue with both the Dynamic and the Moral models. In this line of thinking, emotional distress is not caused by deep dynamic processes that must be exposed, nor can the person's pattern of irresponsible choices be blamed for all his problems. The central area of concern is unsatisfying relationships.

To Relational Model counselors, the most significant fact about people is not that they are complicated psychologically or irresponsible morally, but rather that they were made to love and be loved. We were designed for relationship. Consequently we yearn for it. Our deepest parts cry out for intimacy and meaningful involvement with others.

Human problems, in this view, are best understood as defensive attempts to handle the pain of fear and tension in significant relationships. By responding to each other defensively, we minimize the chances of gaining the closeness we legitimately want. The result is a profound loneliness that strengthens our determination to protect ourselves from the hurt we fear. People are caught up in a vicious cycle of hurt, defensive retreat, more hurt, more retreat.

Relational counselors try to provide for their clients an affirming relationship between them that is designed (1) to spark the hope of reduced loneliness through meaningful interaction with at least one other human being, and (2) to offer a safe setting for trying out new, nondefensive patterns of relating.

Values such as openness, courage, vulnerability, and assertiveness are typically emphasized by Relational Model counselors. People need to admit honestly to themselves how they feel around others and to demonstrate the courage to be who they really are. They must give up their manipulative attempts to win affection or avoid rejection and instead present themselves to others without pretense or retreat.

Figure 5.1 summarizes the essentials of each model.

|  | PROBLEM | SOLUTION |
|---|---|---|
| Dynamic Model | Sickness | Treatment |
| Moral Model | Irresponsibility/Sin | Exhortation to Change Behavior |
| Relational Model | Loneliness | Affirmation/Self-Expression |

*Figure 5.1*

Most approaches to counseling reflect the core assumptions of one or more of these three models. Some approaches fall neatly within one model (nouthetic counseling largely follows a Moral Model; Rogerian counseling is Relational in focus; classical psychoanalysis is obviously Dynamic), but others are not so easily categorized.

Behavior therapy, for example, is a curious blend of the Dynamic and the Moral models in its insistence that people are victims of bad environments and its emphasis that what needs to be changed is behavior, not internal structures. Gestalt therapy and its stepchild, primal therapy, reflect a blend of Dynamic and Relational assumptions.

I think there is little to gain in carefully defining each approach in terms of these three models. I do believe, however, that the assumptions central to each model are basic to one's view of people and therefore deserve some thought.

The assumptions we accept will determine what we do when we counsel. Dynamic Model counselors, for example, will rarely advise people to change behaviors. Moral Model counselors give directive counsel freely.

Moral Model counselors spend little time looking deeply into a counselee's past or into her current subtle motivations, but Dynamic Model counselors regard such exploration as crucial to really helping.

Relational Model counselors tend to be less concerned about dependency issues with their counselees than do Dynamic Model counselors, who devote considerable effort to dealing with transference and maintaining a professional distance. The focus of the Relational Model on the relationship between counselor and client as a major instrument of change differs greatly from the Moral Model emphasis on instruction as a tool of counseling.

> The assumptions we accept will determine what we do when we counsel.

The differences between the models are real. And because each model leads us in a different direction when we counsel, it is important that we carefully decide what we believe. These models cannot all be right.

If there is a standard by which all thinking about people, problems, and solutions should be measured, then every viewpoint must be studied in light of that standard. Having already concluded that the Bible is an authoritative and sufficient standard, we can ask, if we begin with the Bible, which model for counseling emerges?

Should biblical counselors look deeply into the personality as Dynamic theorists suggest, or should that sort of deep analysis be marked off-limits to counselors and reserved for the Holy Spirit?

Should biblical counselors deal mostly with changing behavior, perhaps emphasizing prayer, Bible reading, and church attendance as necessary ways to strengthen and guide a person's determination to change? Or does the Bible support a more complex picture of people than is taken into account by those who focus on behavior change?

Should biblical counselors interpret our responsibility to love one another as reason to choose a Relational Model of counseling, or is there a place for deeper introspection and stronger confrontation?

Which model is biblical? One more than the others? Two of them? A blend of all three? Or another model entirely? This is the concern of the next chapter. We will begin by dealing with the question "Who are we?"

*Chapter 6*

# People Bear
# the Image of God!

Several years ago, I spent some time wandering through the long corridors of the psychology section in a major American university. One very large part was devoted to books that dealt with the study of human nature. Literally thousands of volumes were filled with the varied and often contradictory ideas of thoughtful men and women who had wrestled with the question "Who am I?"

I remember feeling a sense of deep helplessness sweep through me as I continued to thumb through the pages. Does anybody know? Can the question be answered with reliable authority, or must we resign ourselves to being the product of imaginative speculation? Can I ever know who I really am, who my wife and children are, what my clients are really like?

It will not do to dismiss these questions as too philosophical and then to insist on a return to more practical matters. Who we are is an enormously important and, in the long run, a thoroughly practical concern. Every effort to help people live responsible, productive, and joyful lives assumes some position or other on that question.

When counselors encourage the release of repressed emotions, they are assuming something about human nature that supports the idea that emotional expression is a healthy thing. When other counselors work to replace negative cognitions with healthy ones in an attempt to relieve depression, they are accepting the theory that conscious mental processes under our direct control are central to how we function.

Counseling theory always begins, either explicitly or implicitly, with a set of very basic ideas about human nature. And these ideas serve two functions: they represent boundaries within which we can develop a model of counseling, and they act as catalysts to guide our thinking in certain directions. Therefore it is necessary to spell out our viewpoint about human nature before we begin to construct our counseling model.

When we start asking questions about our essential nature, we enter a realm of discourse where intuition, rational thought, and empirical observation quickly prove inadequate. Unless people who know all the answers choose to pass on some of their knowledge to us, we will float about in shifting directions with neither sail nor anchor. Without revelation we are locked up to the uncertainty responsible for thousands of books that cannot reach even a broad consensus about our nature as human beings. We need revelation. The good news is that God has spoken on the subject.

With biblical revelation as my framework, I make two assumptions when I think about people. These assumptions serve for me the dual functions of boundary and catalyst.

First, I assume that *people are similar to God*. The Bible clearly states that we were created in the image of God. Whatever else that may mean, it includes the central idea that in some important respects we resemble God.

Second, I assume that *something terrible has happened that has badly distorted the similarity.* Things within us and within the world are not now as they should be. When Adam and Eve sinned, they disfigured both themselves and all their descendants so severely that we now function far beneath the level at which we were intended. We're something like an airplane with cracked wings rolling awkwardly down a highway rather than flying through the air. The image has been reduced to something grotesque. It has not been lost, just badly marred.

My starting point as I try to understand people is this: People are fallen image-bearers. I accept this premise because the Bible accepts it.

> People are fallen image-bearers.

In Genesis 1, God is spoken of without introduction. He simply is: "In the beginning God ..." (v. 1).

In the same chapter, the first human beings arrive as a special creation whose specialness depends on the fact that they bear God's image.

> Then God said, "Let us make mankind in our image, in our likeness ... So God created mankind in his own image. In the image of God he created them; male and female he created them (Genesis 1:26 – 27).

And because these human beings bear God's image, they are capable of entering into relationship with God: "Then God blessed them and said ..." (Genesis 1:28).

In Genesis 3, humanity's tragic fall into sin is recorded. Relationship is severed, the image defaced. From Genesis 4 through the end of the Bible, humans are regarded as fallen image-bearers, beings marked by both dignity (the image) and depravity (the Fall).

If our understanding of people is to be adequate, we must fully take into account both the beauty of our essential dignity and the horror of our shameful depravity. A biblical model of counseling must take the image of God and the fall of humanity as its starting point, as illustrated in figure 6.1.

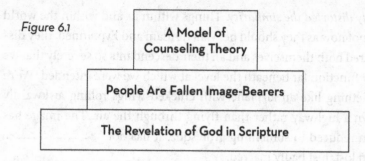

Figure 6.1

**A Model of
Counseling Theory**

**People Are Fallen Image-Bearers**

**The Revelation of God in Scripture**

## The Image of God

The first task is to discuss a question that has generated hot debate for centuries and will likely continue to do so until the Lord returns: What does it mean to be made in the image of God?

My treatment of this topic is not very likely to settle the debate. Instead, I fear that the depth of my discussion will frustrate both the nontheologically trained reader with its complexity and the theologically trained reader with its brevity and incompleteness. I ask for patience from both groups. My purpose is to sketch a few core ideas that will lead us, not into academic controversy, but toward a model of counseling.

Although there are dozens of viewpoints on what constitutes the image of God, four distinct ideas have emerged from the confusion that have won considerable acceptance in various religious circles: Dominion/Representation, Moral Virtue, Amoral Capacity, Similarity. To lay a strong enough foundation to support the rest of my thinking, let me take the time to consider briefly each of these theories.

### 1. Image as Dominion/Representation

To bear the image of God, some contend, means that we act on his behalf in this world, exercising authority over creation as God's representatives. Our responsibility and calling are faithfully to reflect his character and purposes in all that we do.

In Genesis 1:27–28, the Bible records that the members of the

Godhead decided to " ... make mankind in our image,... they may rule ..." The association between God's image and the call to rule has been interpreted as one argument in favor of the view that bearing the image means to have dominion as God's representative.

## 2. Image as Moral Virtue

Martin Luther held the view that the image of God consists in the moral excellence that human beings enjoyed at Creation, lost in the Fall, and can regain in Christ.

The New Testament teaches that for Christians to be restored in the image of Christ means that they are growing in knowledge, holiness, and righteousness (Ephesians 4:22 – 25; Colossians 3:9 – 10). In the view of many, the moral virtues that make up the image of Christ are central to the definition of the image of God in Genesis 1.

Adam and Eve were created with virtue. They were innocent, uncorrupted, good. But since the Fall, human beings have lost all claim to moral excellence. We are now darkened in understanding rather than knowledgeable; sinful in disposition rather than holy; and wicked in behavior rather than righteous.

According to this definition (that is, image equals virtue), the image has been entirely lost. To speak of a tarnished image rather than an obliterated one would suggest that human beings still have some good within them that commends itself to God. But the Bible is clear that all our righteousness is as "filthy rags" (Isaiah 64:6), none of us seeks after God, we have all "gone astray" (Isaiah 53:6).

The image of God, if understood to mean moral excellence in one's character, has been wholly lost, but is recoverable through the gift of God's righteousness and the sanctifying work of the Holy Spirit.

## 3. Image as Amoral Capacity

A third understanding of the image has been developed by Roman Catholic theologians. In their view, when Adam was created he was neither good nor bad. He was a morally neutral being with "lower" appetites that could lead him into trouble. His faculty for reasoning enabled him to see the consequences of letting his appetites control him, but he had no clear moral strength to keep his desires in check.

God graciously intervened on Adam's behalf by granting him an extra measure of grace (referred to as *donum superadditum:* an addition of goodness). Adam was now empowered to act properly whenever his lower appetites collided with his higher reason. But in the Fall he rejected the influence of this extra grace and was reduced to a being controlled by his carnal desires. In order to be "saved" from his fallen state, he needed not only forgiveness, but another supply of grace that he could draw on to live as he should.

The critical point to notice is the understanding of what was lost in the Fall. Adam lost not an acceptable state of moral innocence before God, but rather the extra grace needed to live commendably before God. What must be regained therefore is *not* a new standing of righteousness received as a gift from God. Instead, people need more grace to hold the lower appetites under control. The church, through her sacraments, provides that grace, enabling sinners to develop within themselves the righteousness that a holy God requires.

The effect of this thinking is to weaken the idea of depravity by assuming that human beings are intrinsically morally neutral and just need help to be godly. Sinfulness becomes a moral lapse that can be overcome by right living. Christ's death still figures as the basis for forgiveness, but it must now be coupled with human effort in order for a sinner to achieve right standing with God. This is nothing less than a theology of salvation by works.

We must be careful in our discussion of the image of God to avoid the implication that human beings are morally neutral, equally capable of good or bad. As I shall discuss in a moment, I believe that the image of God refers to the capacities or qualities of personhood, but I hold that these capacities never have existed and never do exist in a moral vacuum. Before the Fall, God said that humankind was good. When Adam fell, he became a corrupted being, in need of both forgiveness and the gift of a righteousness that he could never develop. Once justified by the grace of God alone, we are granted the power to live consistently with our own position in Christ. But our good works do not add to our position of acceptability; instead they are a grateful response to the One who gave us that position.

### 4. Image as Similarity

The fourth view of the image of God holds that our similarity to God is found in the definition of personhood. Both God and humankind possess qualities that distinguish us from nonpersonal beings.

Sometime ago I purchased an antique rolltop desk. The price tag gave clear testimony that the desk was an original, not a recently made copy. I have since seen reproductions of the real thing that looked almost exactly the same. The reproductions have value in that they resemble the authentic original. They are not the original, but they were crafted to be like the original. They were made in the original's image.

In much the same way, you and I are carefully crafted reproductions. We bear the image of God. In certain respects we resemble him. In other respects, of course, there is a gulf of difference as wide and deep as infinity. Theologians speak of incommunicable attributes of God, such as omnipotence or self-existence, which God cannot share with his creation. There are distinctions between God and human beings.

But there are similarities. There are communicable attributes that God has built into his creatures. In his classic book *Knowing God*, J. I. Packer says that when God made human beings, he "communicated to [them] qualities in himself."[1] J. Oliver Buswell states in his *Systematic Theology* that Genesis 1:25–28 means that human beings are "created to resemble God in some important ways."[2]

The obvious question to ask is, in what way (or ways) are we similar to God? Most theologians agree with Lewis Sperry Chafer, who states that "this resemblance is featured in the immaterial and not the material part of [human beings]."[3] The similarity lies not in our appearance, but is deeply etched into the core of our personality. God and the human being are both *persons,* each possessing the characteristics and qualities that combine to make up a person. Animals and trees and rocks are nonpersons, but human beings are persons, like God.

Whatever those characteristics are that as persons we share with God, it seems clear that they have survived the Fall (see Genesis 5:1 – 3; 9:6; 1 Corinthians 11:7; James 3:9). Contrary to the Lutheran view, Chafer indicates that "though much is said throughout the Bible of [human] sinfulness and of the depths to which [we have] descended, it is not said that [we have] lost the image of God." In fact, he says, the Bible teaches that fallen humanity "retains the image and that it is this reality which determines the extent of [human] degradation."[4]

Reformed theologian Louis Berkhof agrees that the image has not been lost. He teaches that the image of God includes elements that belong to our "natural constitution." These include intellectual power, natural affection, and moral freedom. "As created in the image of God," he writes, we have "a rational and moral nature which [we] did not lose by sin and which [we] could not lose without ceasing to be [human]." He concludes that "the image has been vitiated by sin but still remains ... even after [our] fall into sin."[5]

We may summarize the matter this way: the image of God consists in the enduring qualities of personhood that both God and people share, qualities that define what it means to be a person rather than a nonperson.

Before we think through what these qualities are, let me briefly contrast this view of the image of God with the other three already presented.

The human responsibility to exercise dominion as God's representatives defines not the image itself but rather what human beings are called to do as image-bearers. Because we are persons who can think, choose, and feel, we are capable of ruling over God's creation as his ambassadors. Dominion is made possible because of the image; it is not the image itself.

Neither can moral virtue be made equivalent to the image. As persons who bear God's image, we have chosen to rebel against God (something a non-image-bearer could not do; only image-bearers choose). We have therefore lost any claim to moral virtue, but we remain persons — corrupt and wicked to be sure, but still persons. God, as a gracious Person, has chosen to deal kindly with we who bear his image by redeeming us and restoring us not to *personal similarity* (we never lost that), but to *moral similarity* (the image of Christ as made known in the New Testament).

The elements of personhood that define the image of God must not be regarded as morally neutral capacities that at one time existed in a state of neither good nor evil. From the time of human creation until now, there has never been an act that has not been moving in either a moral or an immoral direction. Everything done is in motion, and the motion is either toward God and therefore good, or away from God and therefore bad. There is nothing morally neutral about us. As personal beings with the capacity to move, we are always subject to moral evaluation.

## The Capacities of Personhood

We are persons. God is a person. We are like him in that we possess the elements that together make up personality. But what are they? What exactly are the capacities of personhood that constitute the image of God?

To answer this question we must draw implications from the Scriptures rather than rely on specific passages. There is no text that begins: "Thus saith the Lord: the elements of personhood are...." We are required therefore to consider how God presents himself in Scripture and to look not only for those elements that distinguish him as the sovereign, infinite God, but also for those qualities that define him as a person.

At the same time, we need to ask whether the qualities we identify are communicable and whether they have in fact been communicated to us. When we can list the distinctions of personality that both God and human beings share, then we will have a basic definition of the image of God.

Here is a summary of the similarities between God and human beings. Each of these concepts will be explored more fully in the next four chapters.

### 1. Deep Longings

In Hosea 11:8, God laments the waywardness of his children in moving terms. The rich, passionate language ("How can I give you up?... My heart is changed within me.") suggests the existence within his personality of a subjective reality not easily defined as merely an emotion. It is deeper than that. With all the intensity of his being, God is longing for the restoration of relationship with his children.

The psalmist describes himself, too, as a personal being who deeply longs. His desire for God is similar to a thirsty deer who pants for water (Psalm 42:1). In another place the psalmist says, "I thirst for you, my whole being longs for you" (Psalm 63:1).

The word for "pants" in Psalm 42:1 literally means a desire so intense that it is audible. The longing is too deep to be dismissed as an emotional reaction to a particular circumstance. Something within human beings is capable of longing for satisfaction in the deepest parts of the personality. Both God and humankind have the capacity to long deeply.

### 2. Evaluative Thinking

In the days of Noah, God evaluated the lives of people. We're told in Genesis 6:5 that "The Lord saw how great the wickedness of the human race had become on the earth, and that every inclination of the thoughts of the human heart was only evil all the time." God thought about humankind and formed his conclusions.

Human beings, too, were thinking. They were looking at their world and developing a set of ideas by which to guide their lives. Although their thoughts were "only evil all the time," still they were thoughts, with direction.

Both God and humans think. They arrive at conclusions that determine their intentions.

### 3. Active Choosing

God "purposes" to do certain things. Whatever he does is according to his purpose, which is directed by the "counsel of his will" (Ephesians 1:9-11 NASB).

Humans are treated as responsible beings, capable of setting a direction and pursuing it. In Philippians 2:12-13 we are instructed to live in consistency with the truth of our salvation by both "willing" (setting a direction) and "working" (pursuing that direction), knowing that whatever good choices we make are empowered by God.

Both God and human beings can choose particular goals to pursue, and they can choose specific actions designed to reach those goals. Persons can actively choose.

### 4. Emotional Experiencing

Our Lord felt sadness when Lazarus died (John 11:33-36). He felt anger when the temple became a commercial sideshow (John 2:14-17). He is pleased when we do his will (Hebrews 13:21). As God interacts with his world, he experiences emotions.

Nehemiah sat down and wept when he heard that Jerusalem's walls were in ruins (Nehemiah 1:4). In the middle of his struggles, Job was "churning inside" (Job 30:27). Paul spoke of himself as perplexed (2 Corinthians 4:8). As people come into contact with the world, they experience what they bump into with feeling.

God and human beings both feel emotions as they interact with the world. I suggest, therefore, that the image of God is to be defined in terms of four capabilities:

- Deeply longing for something personal
- Rationally evaluating what is happening
- Willfully pursuing a chosen direction
- Experiencing one's world emotionally

God has the capacity to long for that which brings him deep joy; so do we. God has the capacity to reflect on his world and evaluate it; so do we. God has the capacity to choose a direction and move accordingly; so do we. God has the capacity to experience feelings self-consciously; so do we.

It must be kept in mind throughout our discussion of these four elements that God is an entirely independent being. He needs no one and nothing in order to function perfectly in all his capacities. On the other hand, we are entirely dependent beings. To use our capacities and to use them with even the smallest degree of effectiveness, we need outside help. We are not sufficient for ourselves, in either our physical or our personal existence. The essence of sin, as we shall consider later, is a refusal to admit our dependence, an arrogant and foolish claim to an independence that simply is not there.

To sum up, God is an independent person with the capacity to long, think, choose, and feel. A human being is a dependent person with the same four capacities. Our beginning framework for understanding people can now be presented simply. Each of us is

— a *personal* being who longs deeply;
— a *rational* being who thinks;
— a *volitional* being who chooses;
— an *emotional* being who feels.

Each of these capacities will be examined for the purpose of developing a comprehensive anthropology that can answer the question, "Who am I?"

## Chapter 7

# Dependent Beings:
# People Are Personal

xploring deeply what goes on inside us can be an intriguing adventure, but it can also be frightening. It is immeasurably more comfortable to probe within ourselves only far enough to solve immediate problems and to restore a pleasant sense of well-being.

When things go wrong that require some sort of handling, most of us feel a little tense. Sometimes the problem is big enough or strange enough to provoke fear, or even terror. Unexplained feelings of depression, recurrent bouts with anxiety that seem to come out of nowhere, or hard-to-resist urges to do something unusual or immoral can be alarming. "What's wrong with me? Am I losing my mind?" are questions asked by scared people, and most of us have asked them at one time or another.

Our sense of responsibility typically leads us to make some attempt at dealing with whatever problems arise. When family tensions erupt into a heated argument or when we feel so angry with our colleagues that we don't bother to show up for a committee meeting, most of us do something to address the problem. Either we pray about it, or try to talk things through with the folks involved, or we do what we think is the right thing to do. But, with a stubbornness not easily shaken, *we tend to avoid looking deeply into ourselves* to evaluate our contribution to the problem.

Why is that so? Why do we rarely attack a problem with a determination to get at the root of things? Do we suspect intuitively that it might be more painful to face the core problem directly than to continue enduring the obvious one? Why do we settle for a level of understanding that, whether accurate or not, gives us the good feeling that at least we're doing something about our problem, but that at the same time shifts attention away from deep parts within us?

Let me illustrate what I'm talking about. A middle-aged husband told me in his second session of marriage counseling, "I think we're communicating now. You were right last time when you pointed out how defensive we both were. You made us think, and we have really made some good progress in opening up to each other. Thanks for getting us on the right track. I think things will go pretty well now."

I turned to his wife and asked if she shared his optimism. With tears forming in her eyes and a trace of anger in her otherwise sad voice, she answered, "I hope so. I'm not sure if I'm feeling all that I wish I were feeling. Some things I just couldn't say to him — I'd be too scared." Her husband glared at her in angry disbelief.

Another man — a pastor — wanted to talk about his teenage daughter who had recently been slipping into depression. Grades were dropping, she was associating with "undesirable" friends, and her attitude toward spiritual things was cool.

The father shared, "I think the real problem is peer pressure. She has a poor self-image, probably because she's taller than most girls — she's always been sensitive about that. I think that makes her more concerned with group acceptance than she ought to be. Our plan is to keep a tighter rein on who she spends time with and to get her more involved with the youth group in our church. She says she doesn't like our new youth pastor, but I think that's part of her bad attitude right now toward the Lord. I wanted your input to see if you might suggest some additional steps that would be helpful."

I suggested that we might look more closely at relationships within the family (including the husband-wife relationship) because tensions in one member often reflect difficult patterns of relating among others. The pastor stiffened, his wife (who had said nothing during our first fifteen minutes of interaction) looked away from us both, and our conversation was cut short when the pastor remembered a meeting he needed to attend. When I wondered out loud if they felt uncomfortable with the prospect of discussing their family life, they both smiled and said no as they hurried out.

Most of us simply are not good at observing ourselves and reflecting honestly on what we see. There is an almost reflexive resistance to asking if perhaps we are haughty or defensive or resentful or scared or controlling. We quickly feel uncomfortable when someone interrupts a perfectly pleasant social chat by offering to give us direct feedback about how we come across to others. Even clear expressions of warm feelings that come from deep parts within us are sometimes hard to force out of our lips, and even more difficult to respond to from others.

> Most of us simply are not good at observing ourselves and reflecting honestly on what we see.

Why? We all know that the human personality is rich and fascinating. As creatures made in God's image, we know there is more to us than a collection of responses to external stimulation. Those of us who believe that humankind is fallen have reason to expect that much of what comes between the stimulus and the response will prove to be ugly and twisted.

We are more than morally neutral machines who function according to predictable laws of nature. Broken machines can be fixed by technicians who are able to make sense of a repair manual.

There is no point to reflecting deeply on the essential nature of a refrigerator that won't stay cold. Just figure out how it works, find out what is broken, and repair it.

But people aren't like that. We're more than impersonal parts of a fixed order. To understand people and to "fix" them when they are broken, we must probe into the way they think and feel. We must study confusing topics like motives and attitudes and the effects of early influences on adult functioning.

The very thing that must be done if we are to understand people is the thing that is most strongly resisted. Especially among Christians. I've heard remarks like "All that you counselors want to do is psychoanalyze everybody. People would be better off spending more time in God's Word and getting their minds off themselves."

A professor in a Christian college recently commented, with some emotion, to a student studying counseling, "I see no need for this emphasis on counseling in the church. If people would just do what the Bible says, their lives would straighten out."

Of course they would. But helping folks do that with their heart, mind, and soul is no easy task. This professor fails to understand that counseling is nothing more than part of discipleship (it is not designed to replace obedience with self-awareness). But more than that, he also is reflecting the common resistance to self-examination that pervades our Christian communities.

Why is a deep inward look not a natural part of all Christian growth? Why is it avoided and sometimes condemned as self-centeredness? I think the reason is simply fear. We fear the unknown; we fear losing control; we fear spoiling a comfortable existence; we fear facing unpleasant truths about ourselves; we fear confusion that robs us of certainty in our decisions.

Many people, upon receiving counseling, have admitted how terrified they were to start. One counselee expressed the feelings of scores of others when she said, "I was afraid to really look at myself. I was scared I might find out some things I wouldn't be able to handle."

Most of us live with a vague fear that something is happening within us that, if we faced it, would ruin whatever comfort we enjoy. The attitude seems to be: However things are, good or bad, they could be worse; so leave well enough alone. Don't poke around beneath the surface of life.

Think of the great many things we deliberately shove into the recesses of our attention. Perhaps it is the shallowness of the relationship we hoped would be richly satisfying. Sometimes it is the aching emptiness that drains life of its color and leaves us with a dull grayness that nothing can brighten.

Maybe it is the true feelings we have toward our children: disappointment that our daughter isn't academically gifted—more average than exceptional; or resentment toward our son for not cooperating to fulfill our expectations of him. And in a dark place we dare not enter, we feel guilt and fear that maybe we're badly failing our kids.

At other times we deny the impression given by our mates that we're not that well liked. Occasionally an urge to do something terrible grips our stomachs, like harming our child or running away, and we pretend it's not there.

The human personality is a reservoir of the most incredible feelings and ideas. But in many circles, especially Christian ones, the message seems to be: Ignore it, keep it out of your mind, focus on Christ in a way that blots out any deep self-awareness.

When that advice is followed, the result is an ostrich-like peace that equips us to relate only to fellow pretenders. Everyone whose head is in the sand can join in a fellowship of contrived contentment. But that sort of peace is entirely different from the peace of God. God's peace can keep our hearts and minds intact while we face whatever may be true about us or about our world.

I am convinced that much of what we admire as spiritual maturity is a fragile adjustment to life built squarely on the foundation of denial. Many people get along quite well because they refuse to acknowledge and grapple with whatever part of reality may be upsetting, especially those parts within themselves. (Internal reality is more easily denied than external reality.)

Is that a wise plan for handling life? Is it a biblical means for promoting contentment? Is denial good? Was Paul encouraging a form of denial when he told us to dwell only on beautiful things (Philippians 4:8)? Or is denial bad? Before I can invite you to look deeply into the human personality, these sorts of questions deserve some attention.

## The Problem With Denial

I must be careful to define my terms, for I believe there is a good form of denial. Chosen denial — a temporary retreat from stress for purposes of restoration and regaining perspective — is necessary and desirable. I am not at all opposed to vacations, or to occasional breaks from caring for sick relatives or from parenting three active children, or from being hospitable to lonely friends. We all need relief from stressful responsibilities.

When I speak of denial, I am concerned with *the idea that maturity comes from not thinking too deeply about oneself.* Christ's call to deny ourselves is sometimes taken to mean that we should not spend time trying to understand what is happening within us. If we feel depressed, we must not wonder what motives or feelings might be involved. We should simply read God's Word, claim appropriate promises, and do what we're told to do. Reflection about oneself is regarded as an unhealthy, introspective focus on self rather than on Christ and is therefore unbiblical. To reach maturity as this line of thinking defines it requires us to deny many things inside us.

This sort of denial is wrong on at least two counts: (1) it contributes to the idea that the solution to a problem is to go around it, not through it; therefore the resources of God become useful in skirting problems, not solving them; and (2) the Bible expressly states that

God has built us with the ability to explore our deepest parts.

> The human spirit is the lamp of the LORD
>> that sheds light on one's inmost being.
>
> PROVERBS 20:27

God intends for us to explore our inmost being so that truth may be lodged deeply within us.

> Yet you desired faithfulness even in the womb;
> you taught me wisdom in that secret place.
>
> PSALM 51:6[1]

Although our hearts are deceitful so as to become unknowable, God sees everything clearly. He grants whatever knowledge we should have through (1) his Word, (2) his Spirit, and (3) his people (Jeremiah 17:9 – 10; Hebrews 4:12 – 13; Hebrews 3:13). Therefore we can *expect* to become aware of those hidden issues that are blocking our growth if we vulnerably and humbly present ourselves before God with an attitude of "Search me!" (Psalm 139:23 – 24).

It is true that there are real dangers and risks in looking intently inward. A serious loss of balance can result. We can become morbidly preoccupied with our own inner workings to the point where we see ourselves as specimens to be studied rather than as image-bearers who should obey. Truths about ourselves that should be convicting may come to provoke only intrigue and fascination.

A deep look inside can weaken our sense of personal sin (the very opposite of what it should do) and feed our deceptive tendencies. Rather than generating an awareness of subtle sin, continual self-examination can lead to self-centeredness that masquerades as a holy struggle to go deeper with the Lord.

As a caution against such abuses of looking inward, we must remember that the essence of holiness is other-centeredness, a worshipful love for God and a love for others that motivates sacrificial care for them. Godly self-examination has an outward and forward look. Although it may take us through periods of internal pain and self-loathing as previously denied realities are exposed, there must

> The essence of holiness is other-centeredness, a worshipful love for God and a love for others that motivates sacrificial care for them.

be the clear commitment to *use* whatever is discovered to become more like the Lord, to deal aggressively with whatever is wrong.

Introspection can become a means of avoiding rather than assuming responsibility. It has the potential to promote a gloomy, cynical negativism by reminding us more of our wretchedness than of the Savior's beauty. And that is bad. Encouraging people to look honestly at themselves and to give up denial as a coping strategy is risky business. There are dangers to reckon with and cautions to observe.

But (and this is an important "but") denial has its own set of dangers. The insistence that we keep our eyes off ourselves and on Jesus too often reflects a desire to enjoy the level of comfort that only denial provides.

There is, of course, comfort in Christ. But it is never a comfort that depends on pretense. Paul knew the comfort of Christ in the middle of recognized and experienced suffering, both internal struggle and external persecution. His joy was not built on denial. Looking away to Jesus never requires that we deny the reality of what may be happening around and within us. Nor does it require minimizing the sheer ugliness of some parts of reality.

When the Jews in the wilderness were bitten by snakes, it was precisely because they first looked at themselves that they then looked up to the brass serpent for help (Numbers 21:4–9). Recognition of our desperate plight provides urgent motivation to look away from ourselves and to turn in dependence to Jesus. It is *good* to know who we are.

Perhaps I can summarize my thinking in a single thought: *The*

*whole point of self-exploration is to learn that we are dependent beings
whose life requires union with God.* As long as we think our problems
are well in hand, our natural commitment to independence remains
strong. Such is the nature of fallen people. But when we are gripped by
an overwhelming sense of helplessness in the face of things we simply
cannot handle, our misplaced self-confidence is badly shaken. Grateful trust becomes an attractive option. *Biblical counseling involves an
uncovering of what has been deeply hidden for the purpose of promoting
the simple but profound awareness that we need God; we need his forgiveness, his power, his life.* Therefore it is good and necessary for real
spiritual growth to face what we are most inclined to deny.

Image-bearers need God. Fallen image-bearers believe they
are sufficient for themselves. We think we can manage to make life
meaningful without revolving our lives around God. We cannot. But
we *think* we can. And that's why God calls us "foolish" (1 Corinthians 1:20): we believe something that is wrong, foolish, inconceivable,
and absurd. The great task of reversing the effects of the Fall requires
on our part that we come to terms with our utter dependency. As we
study ourselves, we can judge whether we are seeing things clearly
by the sense of desperate need that emerges. The more accurately we
see ourselves, the more dependent we realize ourselves to be.

But that is precisely what we are committed to avoiding. Admitted dependency provokes in us the fear of absolute vulnerability, a
radical out-of-controlness at a level where we demand that we be in
control.

As we journey into the personal core of our being, we must
expect to feel both resistance and confusion, for we will encounter
things that are hard to face, that hurt and convict. Perhaps we will
remain clinical as we reflect on our deepest parts; it is safer to be a
student thinking about a hypothesis than a person confronting his
or her own reality. But with a commitment to know God as deeply as
we can (one taste makes us want another) and with an implicit trust
in Scripture as our guide, perhaps we can face ourselves in a way

that will free us to love the Lord more deeply than ever before and to share that love more eagerly with others.

In our look inside, I rely heavily on two biblical concepts to point the way: (1) the concept of innermost being, and (2) the idea of our soul's deepest thirst.

## Innermost Being

In John 7:37–38 Jesus invited all who were thirsty to come to him. He promised that for those who come he would fill a central part with life—unique, deeply satisfying, permanent, and available only in him.

> Let anyone who is thirsty come to me and drink. Whoever believes in me, as Scripture has said, rivers of living water will flow from within them.

That life, Christ said, would penetrate into the core of our being. Somewhere in the center of human personality is our innermost being, a deep part within us from which God causes living waters to flow.

The word Jesus used to refer to this deep part within (the Greek word *koilia,* which some versions translate "belly") literally means an open space or cavity. It can refer to the stomach, as in Matthew 12:40 where we're told that a fish's belly housed Jonah for three days and nights. But the same word can be used metaphorically to mean a void, an empty space that can be and desperately longs to be filled. Each of us has what I like to call a Hollow Core in our personality, a central part that is empty but yearns to be filled.

To the degree that this Hollow Core is full, we experience a profound sense of wholeness, an unspeakable joy, an energizing conviction that life makes sense, that we fit, that what we do is important. But when the Hollow Core is empty (or more precisely, when we feel the emptiness — there are ways to numb the feeling), our souls are torn apart with an unbearable ache, a throbbing loneliness that demands relief, a morbid sense of pointlessness that paralyzes us with anger, cynicism, and frustration.

The Lord appeals directly to this deep ache in our core, promising to do for us what no psychologist can ever hope to do. Jesus offers us deep, thorough, lasting satisfaction that affirms our identity and at the same time frees us from self-centeredness. Christ offers life, a Full Core. It is tragic and sad that so many professing Christians sing praises with a trumped-up fullness designed to convince themselves and others that they're doing quite well. There really is very little of the reality of life visible in our Christian communities or felt in the hearts of believers.

> Each of us has what I like to call a Hollow Core in our personality, a central part that is empty but yearns to be filled.

Two other passages shed important light on the Hollow Core and how it functions. Romans 16:18 speaks of people who are slaves, not of Christ, but of their own *innermost being* (*koilia*). In Philippians 3:19 Paul warns his readers about enemies of the cross whose god is their appetite or *innermost being* — the same word again.

Apparently this dimension in our personality is a force to be reckoned with. Either it is the place where God's Spirit fills us with a vital, rich life, or it becomes a monstrous power that relentlessly controls the core direction of our lives. When Christ's invitation to come is ignored, we eventually become driven people, hopelessly committed to a futile search for fulfillment.

Nature, whether physical or personal, abhors a vacuum. Internal emptiness becomes an absolutely compelling force that drives people to sacrifice anything, eventually even their own identities, in an effort to find themselves.

The search for identity is real. Image-bearers were designed to enjoy their clear identity as happy persons who belong to God. Fallen image-bearers, however, are incredibly foolish: we look for fullness every place except where it can be found. No one seeks after God. We all drink from broken cisterns that can hold no water (Jeremiah 2:13). The result is a life lived entirely in the service of oneself, a mad pursuit of whatever holds out the hope of fullness.

Everything people do is moving in a chosen direction. Behavior is never static but always dynamic; behavior is always behavior-in-motion. We all go after whatever we think will give us what we want. To understand people deeply requires that we realize that

— all behavior is moving in a direction toward a chosen goal;
— without the fullness of Christ filling our innermost being, we are motivated to move in whatever direction we think will relieve the emptiness of our Hollow Core.

A model of counseling that fails to come to grips with the Hollow Core by promoting an acute awareness of its emptiness and by clearly presenting the Christian (and only) route to fullness is unbiblical. Symptoms may be relieved, feelings may become more pleasant, a counterfeit sense of well-being may be enjoyed, but if the horrible reality of a Hollow Core remains unchanged, counselees remain slaves to the god of their own longings for satisfaction. We must attack the core problem in the human personality, the real culprit behind all nonorganically caused human distress: *a steadfast determination to remain independent of God and still make life work.*

Counseling that is biblical addresses our arrogant denial of dependency. It brings us into touch with the truth of our utter dependency by stripping away all pretense to independence, a painful process that is absolutely necessary if true maturity is to be realized. Yielding control of arranging for our own satisfaction is frightening. It puts us in the position of facing utter emptiness unless someone else comes through. And fallen human beings would prefer to keep control of their own destiny, though we are impotent, rather than trust in the "uncertainty" of a faithful and good God.

The emotional problems we human beings experience have a moral root. Although in most cases they are not the product of immediate, conscious, willful sin, their basis can be found in a life-long (and often unconscious) commitment to depend on our own maneuvering to protect ourselves from feeling the pain of a Hollow Core. Until we pull away the wrappings that hide the moral core of our difficulties, we will not be dealing with the real issues responsible for human suffering.

• • •

So far our search within has discovered a Hollow Core, a longing for satisfaction that will prompt us either to turn in humble dependency to Christ or to rely arrogantly on our own resources to find satisfaction. The next question is obvious: exactly what do we long for? What is the hollowness of the Hollow Core? And what fills it up? The answer lies in my second concept, the thirst that is in our souls.

## Our Thirsty Souls

The Scriptures are full of individual threads woven through its pages to form from a jumble of colors one beautiful tapestry. Threads like "priesthood," "sacrifice," and "the throne of David" make interesting and profitable study. There is one thread that in my thinking deserves much closer attention than it usually receives. That thread is the concept of "thirst." The biblical writers repeat over and over the idea that people are thirsty. Consider just a few of the many passages where the thirst of our souls is the major theme.

As the deer pants for streams of water,
    so my soul pants for you, my God.
PSALM 42:1

119

The word *pants* suggests a deep longing for something the human soul yearns for, comparable in intensity to an animal's craving for water during a prolonged drought. The plain thought is that people long for life, a richly satisfying, internal reality that goes far beyond mere survival.

> Come, all you who are thirsty,
>> come to the waters;
> and you who have no money,
>> come, buy and eat!
> ... eat what is good,
>> and you will delight in the richest of fare....
> listen, that you may live.
>
> ISAIAH 55:1 – 3

Notice that the appeal to come requires a prior awareness of one's thirst. It follows that our desire to know God and to enjoy him depends on a painful awareness of what we lack. Thirst, it should be remembered, is never pleasant. It's the drinking (and its anticipation) that we enjoy. It is therefore right to promote an awareness of what we long for but don't have in order to strengthen our desire for the Lord. When the hungry boy catches a whiff of a fresh-baked apple pie, he loses interest in the ball game and heads for home.

Notice further in the Isaiah passage that people are encouraged to avoid whatever fails to satisfy and to delight in an abundant supply of that which brings real joy. At first glance this seems to contradict the dozens of biblical exhortations to put the interests of others above our own. The Scriptures acknowledge that we all long deeply for satisfaction without ever hinting at a rebuke for our feeling those desires. We must say it clearly: it is not wrong to desire deep joy in our souls. A longing for happiness does not make us selfish. To deny self does not require that we stop caring whether we're happy or not, or that we somehow must nobly rise above an interest in our own well-being.

Selfishness, self-centeredness, and self-indulgence have their roots, not in the longings of our soul, but rather in our arrogant determination to act independently of God in the pursuit of satisfaction. In Jeremiah 2:13 the prophet does not condemn the people for their thirst, but for their attitude of proud self-sufficiency reflected in the digging of their own wells.

> Then Jesus declared, "I am the bread of life. Whoever comes to me will never go hungry, and whoever believes in me will never be thirsty."
>
> JOHN 6:35

Far from condemning our hunger and thirst as self-oriented, our Lord appeals to them as good reason for coming to him. As in John 7:37 – 38, he invites us to forsake all other routes that promise joy and to turn to him for satisfaction of all that our heart longs for. All false routes to joy, it should be noted in passing, have one thing in common: they represent strategies for living that in some measure we can control. They do not require us to yield our core commitment to independence. God's message is consistent: complete trust in another is the route to satisfaction.

Let me summarize a few thoughts. In each fallen image-bearer there is a Hollow Core. This core is the center of thirst, just as the deer's parched throat is the place where the craving for water is felt. The Hollow Core is experienced as a deeply personal thirst, a yearning for something that we cannot satisfy in and of ourselves. So we must ask, exactly what are we longing for?

### Thirst for What?

If unsatisfied people are driven to find relief from the pain of thirst, and if Christ wants to free us to live for him by quenching that thirst, then it seems natural to wonder what it is we all want so badly. The Scriptures, however, seem quiet on the subject. Paul does not write a letter to a local church to clear up confusion about what the

Lord meant when he invited thirsty people to come. Thirst is never defined. What then are we to do?

The answer depends on our approach to Scripture. If we permit ourselves to ask only those questions that the Bible *explicitly* answers, we must put aside our questions about thirst and move on to other matters. If we regard Scripture as inadequate for guiding us as we think about some legitimate questions, we will close our Bibles and continue to puzzle over the nature of our thirst. In that case, we would depend on (1) the data we might gather from extensive observations, and (2) our clear-thinking ability combined with a creative, intuitive ability to make sense of what we observed. The result would be a reasonable yet utterly uncertain set of conclusions about this strange but real thing we're calling thirst.

There is another option. If we view the Bible as a sufficient framework for thinking through every important question about people, then we will reflect long and hard on the nature of our thirst, drawing out the implications of biblical data, always remaining within the boundaries that Scripture imposes.

With that understanding (explained in chapters 4 and 5), let me sketch a biblical answer to the question, "What do we thirst for?" I want first to summarize my thinking to show where I am heading and then to consider my argument in more detail.

> We have been made with a capacity to move purposefully in a direction, to join God in his purposes.

Because God is in his very nature a *relational* being (there are three persons in the Godhead, capable of enjoying interrelationships), human beings, created to be like God, are also relational beings. We have been built for relationship with God and with other people. It follows that in the most central part of our being, we long to enjoy what we were designed to experience. We long for *relationship*.

God is more than a relational being, of course. He is also a *pur-*

*poseful* being who unerringly moves toward a chosen end point. History has direction. It is in motion toward a conclusion determined by God. Although sin has corrupted the original design of how things were to work, God is about the business of restoring the order he always intended. We were created to be a part of God's design and, in Christ, we have been re-created to participate in the cleanup campaign. We have been made with a capacity to move purposefully in a direction, to join God in his purposes. We are more than senseless parts of a preordered system that fatalistically moves us along. Therefore, in our innermost being, I suggest that we thirst to be a part of the eternal plan, to make a lasting difference in our world. We long for *impact*.

*Relationship* and *impact*: legitimate thirsts of the human soul. Christians long to obey God because obedience is the condition for intimacy of relationship. We long to minister to others. We feel whole and good when we do. Ministry satisfies our longing for impact.

Relationship and impact are longings deeply embedded in our hearts that put us in touch with our dependency. God, who is thoroughly independent, is sufficient within himself for both relationship and impact. We humans, however, require resources that we can neither generate nor control in order to enjoy the acceptance of loving relationship and the value of sharing in meaningful purpose.

The fact of our dependence was brought home with awful finality when Adam fell. Before he sinned, Adam lived in perfect fellowship with the God on whom he depended. If an angel had stopped by the garden one evening and asked, "Adam, do you long for relationship and impact?" I suspect Adam would have looked rather puzzled and replied, "I'm not sure what you mean. I have God. What more could I want?"

But when God withdrew from Adam because of his sin, that capacity within Adam that enabled him to enjoy God suddenly was empty. The core became hollow. From his innermost being Adam longed for the fullness he lost — but because of his darkened mind, he looked for it everywhere except in God.

Before the Fall, Adam was dependent but complete — and therefore satisfied. After the Fall, the fact of his dependency was realized in his felt incompleteness without God. He was empty. The longings for relationship and impact, though in themselves not sinful, would never have been felt had sin not severed fellowship with God. All Adam's descendants struggle with the grim reminder of our dependency, a core that is hollow because we are separated from God. Fallen human beings are thirsty.

We thirst for the warmth of true love and for the thrill of real meaning. The more we taste the reality of our longings, the more we become aware of our dependency, of the horror of distance from God, of the joy of intimacy with God.

Having traced the course of this thinking, let us look more closely at the nature of our longings.

## Our Longing for Relationship

Begin with the truth that God is a Trinity: three persons, one God. This is certainly a mystery, but it has a clear message: There is relationship within the very nature of God. God is a personal being who exists eternally in a relationship among persons: he is his own community.

When God decided to create a kind of being different from angels, he designed his new creation with a unique ability to respond to his love by choosing to enter into relationship with both him and other similar beings. God created us for relationship with himself and others. We are fundamentally relational creatures. Like babies crying for the milk that sustains physical life, people desperately reach out for the kind of relationship that brings personal health.

Pause for a moment. It is possible, and terribly common, to remain clinical and detached from the reality of our longings even as we discuss them. It is far easier to describe our longings than to experience them. But that won't do. The very nature of our longings requires that they be felt to be properly understood. No academic definition can possibly capture the passion with which we yearn for someone to care. I urge the reader to open up to the idea of literally sensing this deep and powerful desire.

Think about the times people impor-tant to you have let you down. Reflect on the disappointment you felt. Ask yourself

> It is far easier to describe our longings than to experience them.

what you would have wanted that person to say or to do. How would you have felt if your father had warmly said, "I love you," rather than stiffly retreated? What would it have been like if your mother had been sweetly affirming rather than critical? One of the best ways to become aware of your longings is to reflect on the richest dis-appointments you have felt in relationships with significant others and to think through what could have been done that would have touched you with joy.

Let me try to reduce this profound longing for relationship to a simple definition: *Each of us fervently wants someone to see us exactly as we are, warts and all, and still accept us.* Because no other human being can ever see all of us, a nagging doubt clouds even the best relationships: what would they think of me if they knew that ...?

The thought that someone can remain warmly committed to us even with all our faults exposed is utterly inconceivable—yet we long for that experience. We long to be in relationship with someone who is strong enough to be constant, someone whose love is untainted by even a trace of manipulative self-interest, someone who really *wants* us.

As image-bearers we long for relationship. As fallen image-bear-ers, we turn away from God to look for it. No wonder God calls us foolish! To walk past a fountain gushing with clear, cold water when we are thirsty and go instead to a broken fountain with a limited sup-ply of brown, bacteria-ridden, lukewarm water is stupid.

Whenever we turn to anyone other than God to satisfy our deep-est longing for relationship, we *will* be disappointed. Guaranteed!

Not even the best parents in the world or the most loving spouse can give me what I crave: pure, undiluted love.

When we depend on others, we inevitably demand that they respond as we wish. When they fail us, we feel hurt and angry. We begin to maneuver the relationship to keep us safe from more hurt while at the same time working to extract more of what we want from the other. The effect is distance and coolness, the inevitable product of a manipulative approach to relationships. People who were designed to know the joy of relationship feel only the pain of separation and loneliness. How sad!

### The Longing for Impact

I remember attending the funeral of a college professor I deeply respected. In several philosophy courses he challenged me to abandon beliefs that I had merely inherited and to determine which beliefs could win my commitment. He was a clear thinker, a man who listened to my attempts to explain the gospel. He was not, as far as I know, a believer when he died.

At the funeral, our college chaplain (himself a Christian only in a nominal sense) remarked that the large turnout of students and alumni bore eloquent testimony to our appreciation and respect for the deceased professor. The chaplain reminded us of the impact the man had made on our lives by appealing to an illustration that nearly shattered my composure. The professor's life, he told us, was like a series of footsteps imprinted on the sands of time and specifically on our lives. Our purpose in coming to his funeral was to reflect on those footprints until the tide of passing days rolled over the sand and wiped away the imprint forever.

As I heard those words, everything inside me screamed. I remember breathing a prayer that the preacher who conducted my funeral would do better than that, that he or she could truthfully affirm the lasting significance of my life. Deep within my soul is a part that violently rebels at the chaplain's illustration, and that part, I suggest, is my innermost being. I thirst for meaning, for impact, for significance.

We all long for something similar. Maybe the word *adequacy* best describes it. We want to know that we are capable of doing a job that needs to be done. We want to leave a mark on our world, a real and enduring difference that matters.

We experience this desire for impact in many ways. Inspecting a newly waxed car or a freshly cut lawn provides a measure of legitimate satisfaction: "I did it. Because I expended energy, things look better. I made a difference." But there is a problem with the limitedness of this impact.

The dishwasher's observation that clean dishes are quickly soiled reduces the pleasure of getting them clean. Short-lived impact is not terribly exciting. We desire an impact that is important and lasting. Impact ranging from the trivial (well-trimmed lawns) to more important matters (business success or family harmony) provides different degrees of satisfaction, but never enough.

Let me define this thirst for impact as *a desire to be adequate for a meaningful task, a desire to know that we are capable of taking hold of our world and doing something valuable and well.*

We are a thirsty people. We long for relationship and impact, desires that only God can fully satisfy. The concept can be sketched as shown in figure 7.1. In keeping with the idea of an empty space that longs to be filled, let the deep longings of our innermost being be represented by a circle. Let the circle refer to our *capacity* (or thirst) for relationship and impact. The Hollow Core of the human personality is an unfilled personal capacity.

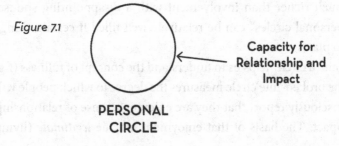

Figure 7.1

Capacity for
Relationship and
Impact

**PERSONAL
CIRCLE**

Because we are *dependent* beings, our capacities are experienced as opportunities for fulfillment that drive us to resources outside ourselves. I am not sufficient for myself. I cannot supply myself with relationship or impact.

Because we are *fallen* beings, our capacities have become desperate longings energized by a fear that we will never find the satisfaction we desire. Had the Fall not occurred, we would know nothing less than unbroken fellowship with God. Our affective experience would be fullness rather than emptiness, joy rather than a chronic ache, and complete relationship rather than aloneness.

But the Fall has happened, and the resultant hollowness of our core drives us to find fulfillment. We cannot escape the longing. To pretend it isn't there is to invite its unnoticed tyranny.

All of us pursue, in one degree or another, avenues of fulfillment that have nothing to do with God. Apart from the Spirit's prompting, none of us would ever seek after God. In Jeremiah 2:13 the prophet indicts God's people for depending on broken cisterns in their efforts to quench thirst, cisterns that they made themselves but that can hold no water. Nothing that human beings can control will ever provide deep satisfaction. Yet we insist on trying to control our own lives. And that fact defines our foolishness.

But our foolishness is not immediately apparent. Even wells with holes in them can hold some water for at least a while. Temporary satisfaction is available in the pleasures of sin. Impressing a friend with our wit or a congregation with our maturity can be exhilarating. Involvement with a person who takes the pressure off feels much richer than involvement with a disappointing spouse. Our "personal circles" can be relatively well filled if certain things fall into place.

Again, a circle helps us to understand the concept of fullness (fig. 7.2). The broken-line circle measures the degree to which people will self-consciously report that they are enjoying a sense of relationship and impact. The basis of that enjoyment may be *legitimate* (living according to godly motivation) or *illegitimate* (drinking from hand-made cisterns before the water runs out).

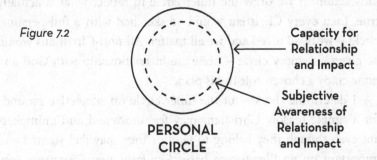

Figure 7.2

Capacity for
Relationship
and Impact

Subjective
Awareness of
Relationship
and Impact

**PERSONAL
CIRCLE**

Satan is a master of counterfeit. He provides almost limitless opportunities for illegitimate but very convincing satisfaction. He capitalizes on our desperate desire for a quick fix to blind us to the long-term emptiness of following him.

There is no worse pain than an empty personal circle — we feel empty, worthless, unloved, and useless. And that pain demands relief. Satan warmly cooperates with our demand by offering us the means to feel better in a hurry. He invites us to become consumed with the purpose of finding relief. When he hooks us, we quickly feel the strength of sin's enslavement.

Life then becomes an effort to gain love and to find means of impact. The purpose of loving God and others and the mission of promoting God's program gets swallowed up in self-centered preoccupation with *my* fulfillment.

Christian joy, it must be remembered, is always a by-product of following Christ. It is not an end in itself. It is not available to people who demand satisfaction on their own terms. God invites us to experience fullness, but the terms are inflexibly his. Those who try to fill the personal circle on their own will lose their lives as they work to find it. Those who lose their lives by pursuing the knowledge of Christ at whatever cost will find the down payment of the relationship and impact for which their soul thirsts.

Notice that the size of the inner circle is determined not by the fact of relationship and impact, but rather by the felt experience of satisfaction. If we drew the inner circle to reflect what is actually true, then every Christian would be sketched with a full personal circle—we're all loved and we all matter. All non-Christians would be given an empty circle—none are in relationship with God and none enjoy a chosen role in his plan.

I determine the size of the inner circle on subjective grounds for a simple reason: Christians may feel unwanted and unimportant even though they belong to God or they may feel wanted and important on an illegitimate basis. Similarly, non-Christians may feel unwanted and unimportant (sometimes a recognition of their true condition) or they may feel wanted and important for illegitimate reasons that don't require God at all.

The range of possibilities is illustrated in figure 7.3.

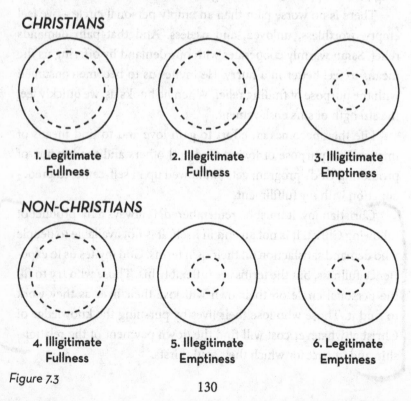

**CHRISTIANS**

1. Legitimate Fullness

2. Illigitimate Fullness

3. Illigitimate Emptiness

**NON-CHRISTIANS**

4. Illigitimate Fullness

5. Illegitimate Emptiness

6. Legitimate Emptiness

Figure 7.3

*Case 1:* A Christian may be growing in his understanding of Christ and eagerly following, to the best of his ability, the path that Christ commands him to walk. At the core of his being, whether circumstances are pleasant or painful, there will be the awareness of God's love and purpose.

*Case 2:* A Christian may pursue objectives on which she is wrongly depending for satisfaction (e.g., respect, appreciation, applause). If she reaches them, she will feel the satisfaction of being accepted and valuable on an illegitimate basis that does not require fellowship with Christ.

*Case 3:* The Christian in case 2 may not reach her objectives. In that case, although she is both loved by God and valuable to God, she will feel neither.

*Case 4:* All non-Christians pursue illegitimate routes to satisfaction. When successful, they feel good about themselves, at least to some degree and for some length of time.

*Case 5:* A non-Christian who fails to reach the objective on which he believes his happiness depends will feel empty for the wrong reasons.

*Case 6:* A non-Christian who realizes that her emptiness is a necessary result of pursuing any goal other than knowing God is experiencing a legitimate emptiness, because it involves a recognition of the necessity of emptiness unless God grants life.

The point to remember is that the size of the inner circle within the personal circle says little about a person's spiritual condition. People may be legitimately full or empty, or illegitimately full or empty. The personal circle is meant to depict two things:

1. We all have the capacity (and longing) to experience relationship and impact — the outer solid circle;

2. We are all aware at any given moment of whether or not we are enjoying a sense of well-being. That sense of well-being (or its absence) may be built on a legitimate or an illegitimate basis — the inner broken circle.

One more concept is needed to complete the personal circles. People have deep longings that can be satisfied only in Christ, and we also have less deep but still very real longings that God does not directly satisfy.

Draw two concentric circles around the personal circles (fig. 7.4). Let the outer one refer to casual longings and the middle one to critical longings. The inner circle represents the personal circle, those crucial longings for relationship and impact that only God can touch completely.

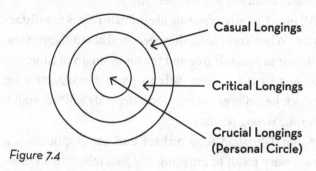

Casual Longings

Critical Longings

Crucial Longings
(Personal Circle)

*Figure 7.4*

*Casual longings* are desires for convenience, comfort, and personal preference. We prefer that it not rain on a holiday, that our car function without breakdown, and that the basement not leak. These can be legitimate desires that we try to realize through prayer and whatever precautions we can take. But when our happiness depends on the satisfaction of casual longings, we are badly out of touch with the deeper desires of the soul.

*Critical longings* include legitimate hopes for deep human relationships and for visible impact on our worlds. We want to see unsaved relatives come to know Christ, sick relatives regain their health, wayward children straighten out, unresponsive spouses give deeply of themselves, and ministry efforts be blessed. These longings are important to us, and rightly so. If these longings go unmet, there are serious consequences: we hurt, we grieve, we ache. But again, if our joy rests entirely on the satisfaction of these very real longings, we have not entered into the potential of life with God.

*Crucial longings* are the deep thirsts of our inmost being. It is a mistake to think that what satisfies our casual or critical longings can ever fully satisfy the core longings of our heart. Only Christ can fill our inmost being with joy. An awareness of these longings does not reduce the pain of unsatisfied longings at other levels; but it does drive us to Christ in utter dependency no matter what else may happen.

Several conclusions can be drawn from the concepts developed in this chapter.

1.  God appeals to people to enter into relationship with him on the basis of their longings. Therefore, knowing what our longings are and experiencing them deeply is important. Those who are not in touch with their longings will not be drawn to the source of their satisfaction.

2.  In their right mind, human beings will pursue God as the source of satisfaction. But we are not in our right mind; no one seeks after God. And that failure to pursue God reflects humanity's foolishness.

3.  Whatever we turn to in order to find satisfaction becomes our god. Our determination to fill the Hollow Core becomes our tyrant, and we revolve our lives around whatever we wrongly believe will provide the fullness we desire.

4.  Satisfaction found in a false god will inevitably lead to a breakdown in relationships. We become demanding rather than sacrificial, self-occupied rather than other-centered (James 4:1 – 3).

## Summary

People are not merely machines that behave or computers that think or sensual organisms that feel. We are *persons,* beings who long deeply for personal satisfaction. The throat of our soul is parched, thirsty for the water of loving relationship and meaningful impact.

We legitimately long for these two kinds of "water," which only God can supply. Everything else is like fizzy, sweet soda: it tastes good going down, but it doesn't touch the thirst.

When we refuse to turn to God for the water he provides, our longings become tyrants, urging us to find satisfaction any way and anywhere we can. The effect is to confirm us in self-centeredness and to strengthen our willingness to violate any moral standard to gain what we desire. We lose our ability to love and to give.

In Christ there is freedom. He provides a satisfaction that liberates us to respond in gratitude to him and in ministering concern to others. The truth of what he provides sets us free from enslavement to our thirst and enables us to live for the glory of God.

Now if all that is true, why do thirsty people walk right by the well of living water and dig their own wells, which at best offer only temporary refreshment? It makes no sense — until we understand how darkened our capacity to think has become. And that brings us to the second capacity of personhood: a rational capacity that has been darkened.

> When we refuse to turn to God for the water he provides, our longings become tyrants, urging us to find satisfaction any way and anywhere we can.

*Chapter 8*

# Foolish Thinkers:
# People Are Rational

ounselors must recognize that the clients they are trying to help
bear the image of God. No other fact is more significant and
necessary to a proper understanding of people.

In the previous chapter I developed the idea that image-bearers are *relational* beings in the way that God is relational. He deeply enjoys loving relationship within the Godhead and longs to enjoy intimacy with his creatures. We were designed with the capacity to be satisfied with his love and to return it by loving him and others.

I suggested also that God, as a personal being, is *purposeful*; that is, he forms a plan and pursues it. Like him, we are purposeful beings who figure out strategies to reach the goals we set for ourselves.

We resemble God in these ways. He is personal (relational and purposeful), and so are we. But, of necessity, we are unlike God in one fundamental way. He is an infinite, completely self-sufficient, entirely independent Being; but we are finite and dependent on God for everything that is needed to sustain life, both physical and personal. We simply do not have the resources within ourselves or the power to command resources elsewhere that we need to enter into loving relationships or to pursue meaningful plans.

> We are thoroughly dependent.
> We depend on someone outside ourselves to give us love and a reason to live.

We are thoroughly dependent. We depend on someone outside ourselves to give us love and a reason to live. Because we were designed for what we do not have (relationship and impact), our very nature yearns for the kind of life we were destined to live. Therefore we long for love and purpose.

When counselors speak with their clients, they must know that they are dealing with image-bearers, persons who cannot be truly alive and happy unless they are in relationship with God and actively and deeply committed to carrying out God's purposes. Every "personal problem" (any problem in living not directly traceable to some organic malfunction) has its ultimate roots in a broken relationship with God and a commitment to a higher priority than knowing God.

If that is true, then counseling should be designed to repair the fractured relationship with God by promoting the sort of repentance that leads to a deep enjoyment of God and an honest commitment to serve him. But most theories of counseling try to effect change without ever dealing with matters of repentance and obedience. And the few theories that do address these matters reduce repentance to a simple decision to conform one's behavior to biblical standards. Deep repentance that concerns itself with the subtle, perverse loyalties of a deceitful heart is rarely involved in most approaches to counseling.

Gestaltists, primal screamers, and memory healers think that real change takes place when people fully experience the pain within. "Self-awareness," "derepression," and "recontextualized memories" are regarded as therapeutic.

Psychodynamic therapy defines the problem as denied conflict that needs to be consciously understood and worked through by facing rather than running from the components of the conflict. The route to change is "insight," which occurs when defenses are penetrated to the point where a person is freed from the uncontrollable effects of disowned conflict.

Existentially oriented therapists think that something in the immediate moment must be grasped. "Realization" is the key. For the secularist, it may be the realization of what is happening between two people as they interact. For the Christian, it may involve a climactic awareness of the reality of Christ, whether through a "second blessing" experience or a grasping of what it means to "reckon oneself dead to sin and alive to Christ."

From the decades-old days of Christian positive thinking and on through the decidedly secular approach of Albert Ellis, known in his day as rational-emotive therapy, today's counselors in large numbers now advocate for cognitive behavior therapy, popularly called CBT. The thread running through these ideas is clear: think unhealthy thoughts and your behavior and emotions will cause you trouble. The solution? Fill your mind with rational, realistic thoughts and you'll feel better and behave more adaptively. For example, after a divorce, don't say to yourself, "I'm a loser. Nobody will ever want me." Think more accurately: "That relationship didn't work. Let me see what I can learn from it and move on."

None of these approaches puts repentance in the center of the change process. There are some, however, that do emphasize sin as the root of all personal problems and have moved toward a focus on repentance and obedience. But too often, sin is defined among these people as nothing more than wrong behavior. Repentance is reduced to a decision to behave differently, and obedience becomes little more than a determination to do what is right. Such efforts are commendable and necessary, but they fail to get at the deep-seated problem of a wicked and deceitful heart.

All these approaches can legitimately claim a degree of effectiveness, sometimes impressive. They all promote change. The vital question, however, is, what kind of change do they promote? Symptom relief, greater feelings of happiness, a reconciled marriage, or an experience of expanded consciousness may all be promoted by different counseling strategies, but are these kinds of changes worthy of image-bearers who were designed for relationship and impact?

Biblical counseling, I submit, must aim toward a unique kind of change. Relief from depression, happier feelings, improved marriages, and more biblical behaviors may be involved in change worthy of an image-bearer, but they do not define it. Image-bearers must change in a way that enables a deeper, worshipful, intimate *enjoyment of God* and a compassionate, penetrating, rich *involvement with others*. Enjoying God and involvement with others — in a word, improved relationships — that's change!

If we are to understand the complexities and difficulties of change, we must have some understanding of the end result of the process. Let me sketch what a changed and continually changing image-bearer looks like. Then we can ask about the process that leads to that kind of change and evaluate proposals for effecting it.

## Healthy People

Healthy people deeply enjoy God, expressed with occasional bursts of ecstasy followed by long periods of quiet allegiance. Their lives are anchored in him. They know that in their deepest parts they have felt his touch.

That touch increasingly liberates them to be more fully involved with others. They are free to enter into other people's lives, openly and vulnerably, with neither protection nor defensiveness, because they are not threatened by the pain of disappointment and conflict that inevitably occurs in rich involvement among fallen people. This inevitable pain does not cause them to back away behind walls of appropriateness ("I'll do what is expected of me") or spiritualized retreat ("Well, we must pray about it"). Mature Christians don't retreat, they increase the level of their involvement.

Healthy people do understand the importance of timing and discretion as they move toward people with whom they experience conflict. And they know, as not-yet-glorified saints, that their efforts at involvement will never be perfectly timed or thoroughly discreet. But still they move toward, not away. Involvement, not retreat, is their lifestyle. And therefore their lives have quiet power. Their very *presence* is felt by a few people in a way that makes them want to live more nobly.

Another reality is that healthy people experience a marred joy. For them, life is lived in the minor key, but with an eager anticipation of the day when the Master Musician will strike up the eternal anthem in the major key. Healthy people are sad because they know things are not now as they should be, yet their disappointment with the world is not expressed in anger. They long for a better day, confident that it will come but groaning until it does.

Healthy people are not afraid of confusion. They have given up their claim to independence and control and can therefore tolerate, even welcome, uncertainty. Confusion deepens their vulnerability to being led by someone who is not confused. They enter warmly into their inherent dependence as finite beings by defining faith as the courage to move on in the absence of clarity.

They struggle — and sometimes fail. They feel some temptations more deeply than less healthy people — and occasionally they yield. But they know what it means to repent from the core of their beings, to tear down the idols to which they looked for satisfaction, and to return to the God of life through whom relationship and impact are available.

Healthy people are not free of the common symptoms of emotional trouble, but the symptoms do not control them, at least not for long. Sometimes they feel profound loneliness and unbearable hurt — and at those times it seems as if they are touching reality more honestly than when they are feeling good. But they go on, aware of a reality yet to be grasped that will replace loneliness with satisfying intimacy and hurt with sheer pleasure. Their styles of interaction with God and others are as varied as snowflakes. But one thing they have in common: a growing ability to be touched by God and to touch others.

That, I suggest, is change worthy of an image-bearer. Even as I write of it, I find myself hungering for more of that kind of life. I want more than freedom from painful memories and repressed emotions. I want more than an understanding of how forces within my unconscious have been shaped in my early years. I want more than changed behavior patterns and relief from troubling symptoms. I want community — community with God and with others. I long for it, with the intensity of a deer panting after water.

Yet what I want the most seems to be in the shortest supply. Many people have the ability to express their feelings and to enjoy certain pleasures in life. But very few enjoy deep relationship with God or others in a way that stirs me to holy coveting.

What's the problem? What needs to be done to move ourselves and others — all people who long for exactly what God richly supplies — toward the source of all that we desire? What is getting in the way of our movement toward him?

## A Shallow View of Sin

The problem is sin, and the remedy is repentance, trust, and obedience. But having said that, we find that the effort to understand the problem and its remedy has merely begun. To discern why thirsty image-bearers walk right past the cool springs of living water to look for satisfaction in the dry sand of the desert, we must understand the foolishness of sin. And we must think deeply.

Perhaps the greatest obstacle to grasping what biblical counseling is all about is a weak and shallow view of sin. Let me quote extensively from *Dynamics of Spiritual Life* by Richard Lovelace. The quotation is long but well worth the space.

> During the last two centuries, the understanding of sin has suffered a correlative decline in the church along with the apprehension of God. The Reformers perceived that fallen human nature was touched in every area by the deforming presence of original sin, the compulsive force operating behind individual acts of transgression. They believed that [human beings have] freedom of will to do as [they] please but that without the renewing work of the Spirit [they are] incurably averse to seeking and serving God. Apart from grace [their] best actions are still built upon the foundation of unbelief and even [their] virtues are organized as weapons against the rule of God....
>
> Although most human beings give the appearance at times of being confused seekers for truth with a naive respect for God,... the reality is that unless they are moved by the Spirit they have a natural distaste for the real God, an uncontrollable desire to break his laws and a constant tendency to sit in judgment on him when they notice him at all. They are at moral enmity with the God revealed in the Bible. Since his purposes cross theirs at every juncture, they really hate him more than any finite object, and this is clearly displayed in their treatment of his son. They are largely unconscious of this enmity. It is usually repressed through their unbelief....
>
> In the eighteenth and nineteenth centuries this deep analysis of sin was abandoned by the growing rationalist movement, which because of its dim apprehension of God began

*Perhaps the greatest obstacle to grasping what biblical counseling is all about is a weak and shallow view of sin.*

to define virtue in ways unrelated to worship and faith in him, and thus to affirm the essential goodness of human nature. During the same period, the church's consciousness of sin began to erode along with its awareness of God. Gradually sin began to be defined in a way which seemed more rationally defensible: *sins are conscious, voluntary acts of transgression against known laws....* [emphasis mine].

During the late nineteenth century, while the church's understanding of the unconscious motivation behind surface actions was vanishing, Sigmund Freud rediscovered this factor and recast it in an elaborate and profound secular mythology. One of the consequences of this remarkable shift is that in the twentieth century pastors have often been reduced to the status of legalistic moralists while the deeper aspects of the cure of souls are generally relegated to psychotherapy, even among Evangelical Christians.

But the structure of sin in the human personality is far more complicated than the isolated acts and thoughts of deliberate disobedience commonly designated by the word. In its biblical definition, sin cannot be limited to isolated instances or patterns of wrongdoing; it is something much more akin to the psychological term *complex:* an organic network of compulsive attitudes, beliefs, and behavior deeply rooted in an alienation from God. Sin originated in the darkening of the human mind and heart as [human beings] turned from the truth about God to embrace a lie about him and consequently a whole universe of lies about his creation. Sinful thoughts, words and deeds flow forth from this darkened heart automatically and compulsively, as water from a polluted fountain.

The human heart is now a reservoir of *unconscious disordered motivation and response, of which unrenewed persons are unaware if left to themselves,* for 'the heart is deceitful

above all things, and desperately corrupt; who can understand it?' (Jeremiah 17:9, RSV).... The mechanism by which
this unconscious reservoir of darkness is formed is identified in Romans 1:18–23 as *repression of traumatic material,*
chiefly the truth about God and our condition.... Their darkness is always a voluntary darkness, though they are unaware
that they are repressing the truth [emphasis mine]."[1]

Several ideas stand out from this passage.

1. Sin is more than wrong behavior.
2. To define sin as nothing more than "conscious, voluntary
   acts of transgression against known laws" is shallow and
   trivializes the awful reality of sin.
3. To understand sin, we must look carefully at the beliefs
   and motives beneath the acts.
4. The beliefs beneath the acts, along with the motivations
   arising from the beliefs, are largely and culpably unconscious (spiritual blindness is desired and therefore chosen).
5. The enlightening and renewing work of God's Spirit is
   necessary if spiritually blind people are to understand the
   deep reality of their sinfulness.
6. Unless we understand sin as rooted in unconscious
   beliefs and motives and figure out how to expose and
   deal with these deep forces within the personality, the
   church will continue to promote superficial adjustment
   while psychotherapists, with or without biblical foundations, will do a better job than the church of restoring
   troubled people to more effective functioning. And that
   is a pitiful tragedy.

Perhaps the major error of evangelical churches today involves a
deficient and shallow understanding of sin such as Lovelace describes.
Many pastors preach an "iceberg view" of sin. All they worry about is

what is visible above the water line. Like a naive sea captain steering a vessel around the tip of the iceberg with no awareness that there is a mountain of ice beneath the surface that could wreck the ship, Christian teachers and disciplers are too often satisfied when their people turn from church-defined sins of misbehavior.

A great mass of sinful beliefs and misdirected motives is never dealt with under that approach. The result is external conformity that masquerades as spiritual health, and internal emptiness and corruption that block the deep enjoyment of God and involvement with others.

The apostle Paul tells us that real change requires far more than altering sinful behavior patterns. Real change demands that we move into the confusing realm of a darkened mind and learn what it means to let the Spirit of God renew us in our essential thinking, as we are admonished in Romans 12:1 – 2.

> Therefore, I urge you, brothers and sisters, in view of God's mercy, to offer your bodies as a living sacrifice, holy and pleasing to God — this is your true and proper worship.
>
> Do not conform to the pattern of this world, but be transformed by the renewing of your mind. Then you will be able to test and approve what God's will is — his good, pleasing and perfect will.

A renewed mind involves far more than memorizing Scripture or meditating on biblical truths, although both are good and desirable. More is required than taking hold of our "thought life" and choosing to remind ourselves of what God has said in his Word, although that too is necessary.

A renewed mind does *not* mean a mind pumped up with exhilarating clichés about the joys of living or our potential to turn tragedy into triumph.

Real change means change in the inner person, where a *deceitful heart*, full of motives hidden even to ourselves, and a *darkened mind*, holding ideas that we may consciously disown, must be exposed and confronted by the message of God.

If sin really includes unconscious beliefs and motives that deny the truth about life in Christ and lead us away from him to other alleged sources of life (wrong ways that lead to death do seem right), then we must look carefully at how we think, what we think, and how our thinking can be renewed.

This is the heart of the second element of personhood as the image of God: the capacity to think.

## The Rational Circle Defined

As image-bearers we resemble God. We do not share his independence, but like him, we have the capacity to observe our world, form impressions of it, organize these impressions into images and beliefs about how our world operates, direct our lives according to our knowledge, and subject our understanding to evaluation and change. In a word, we can think.

*Figure 8.1*

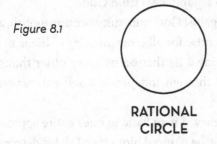

**RATIONAL
CIRCLE**

In creating human beings, God endowed them with rational capacities. Before the Fall, whatever Adam believed, he believed correctly. Before sin entered the world, he in some way perceived himself quite accurately as dependent. He understood that life was in God and that obedience was the basis of relationship between the creature and his Creator.

Adam was not foolish. He knew that he did not have within himself the resources necessary for life; he needed God and he knew it. There was no tug toward independence and self-reliance.

With this accurate understanding of the essential structure of life as the premise, Adam could think objectively and accurately about everything. His mind was neither darkened nor foolish. Let a broken circle reflect the degree to which one's thinking is accurate (fig. 8.2).

Figure 8.2

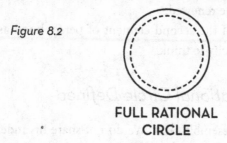

**FULL RATIONAL
CIRCLE**

For reasons that no one fully understands, Adam did the unthinkable: he yielded to Satan's invitation to find a better life than God provided by declaring his independence from God. He rejected the path of dependence, thinking that a superior brand of life was available to him through separateness from God.

With that rebellion against God, humanity became foolish, abandoning the necessary premise for all clear thinking — life is in God, not oneself — and believing a lie that stains every other thought: a better life can be found through independent self-expression and self-determination.

The lie that Adam believed is so basic to one's entire approach to life that, when he bought it, he plunged himself and all his descendants into moral darkness. Humans became rebels against God, believing that obedience to him is neither necessary for life nor required by the fact of who he is and who God is. As Adam's children we naturally think that we can fill our personal circles through our own efforts and resources. But that is not true. Satisfaction is not available except through relationship with God on his terms. Yet we think we know better.

We are committed to independence and, from the core of our being, we move against God. We are at enmity with him. We hate him because he demands what we foolishly think will rob us of life: surrender, trust, and obedience.

Because the very core of our thinking is corrupted with the lie that we can find life apart from God, our beliefs about moral issues are likely to be wrong. We can accurately discern that two plus two equals four in the physical world, but when we try to figure out the moral world we reveal our mental bankruptcy. We are foolish, darkened, and blind. We have an empty rational circle (fig. 8.3).

*Figure 8.3*

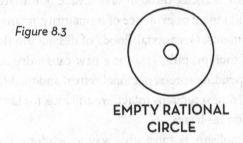

**EMPTY RATIONAL
CIRCLE**

Our foolish thinking, one might suppose, should be self-correcting. When we realize that our ideas on where to find happiness don't work, we should shift to another plan as easily as we change laundry detergent when the advertising claims don't match what we observe in our clothing. And we are flexible — within the limits of foolishness. We shift to whatever alternative plan seems to work unless that plan requires us to compromise our commitment to self-determination.

When a wife refuses to have sex with her husband and scorns him for "thinking of nothing else," replacing her with a warmly cooperative mistress seems to him like a terribly good idea. Movement in that direction (perhaps a weekend affair) confirms the wisdom of the plan. The predictable result is good feelings that provide rich, convincing satisfaction far beyond mere sexual pleasure. Divorce and remarriage may in fact maintain those good feelings for a very long time.

The point is that because there is pleasure in sin for a season (sometimes a long one), illegitimate personal circle pleasure that feels deeply satisfying is available to people who want to live independently. And that's the tricky part; it's Satan's trump card. Independence really does seem to lead to life. The lie of Satan appears to work better than the truth of God. Satisfaction is often felt more immediately in handling things wrongfully than biblically. The saints of Hebrews 11 lived by faith, and many died without enjoying the temporal fruit of their faith.

The longer we continue walking the path of independence, the more deeply we sink into the mud of our corrupted thinking. Hints of emptiness sometimes sneak through and invade our awareness, but we quickly dismiss them as evidence of immaturity, neurosis, or insufficient achievements. Occasional floods of despair are flushed down the drains of therapy, pills, zeal for a new cause, drugs, new forms of pleasure, spending sprees, personal retreat and meditation, or suicide. Our foolishness remains intact; we still look for life without coming to God on his terms.

Somehow this foolishness must give way to wisdom. For the Christian, walking as the unbelievers walk must be increasingly replaced with a new style of living. The staining effects of the Lie (independence means life) must be scoured from the bottom of the personality. Our understanding of life must be continually corrected to conform more and more to the Truth (Jesus Christ is life). Transformation depends on renewing our minds.

## Images and Beliefs

To understand what Paul means when he says that we are to be transformed by the renewing of our minds, we must first determine what activities of our minds need renewal. What precisely goes on in the human mind?

The biblical data do not at first glance seem to provide much help in answering the question. Paul never wrote a systematic description of the "parts" of our personality. He did not draw a psychological road map. Instead he emphasized the *person* — a longing, thinking, choosing, feeling person who can enter into a relationship of loving obedience with God.

But Paul did refer to a number of internal parts or processes that together make up what he calls the "inner being" (e.g., Ephesians 3:16). The "outer being," the visibly behaving person, is represented as the expression of the inner being (heart, mind, soul, etc.). Paul makes it clear that outward change without inward change is worthless. Something inside needs to be altered.

In the same way, our Lord reserved his most scathing criticism for outwardly religious people who were unaffected by the truth of God internally (Matthew 23:25 – 28). People who cleaned up their visible act without dealing with unseen corruption within were singled out as especially worthy of judgment.

The clear message is that if careful attention is not given to internal renewal, external improvement is sheer hypocrisy. Something rooted deep in the center of who I am is desperately in need of change. But what is it that must be renewed?

The longings of the human heart, I submit, cannot be changed. And even if they could, to do so would make humankind less than God designed us to be. Our longings are legitimate. They should be actively felt and embraced in order that we may more richly know God as the Great Satisfier and Lover of the human soul. The problem is not centrally with our longings.[2]

> If careful attention is not given to internal renewal, external improvement is sheer hypocrisy.

In Romans 12:1 – 2, Paul states that the needed renewal must take place within the mind. We direct our lives according to our understanding of who we are and what life is all about. When this understanding is wrong, we will foolishly move in a direction that leads to death.

As rational beings we are able to observe both the world and ourselves and to form pictures of what we see. These pictures gradually develop into *images* of reality, that is, mental representations of how we think things really are.[3]

Not only do we form images of reality that provide a stable framework within which to live, but we also use words to symbolize what we observe in a way that permits us to conceptualize how things work. Over time, our efforts to think things through come together in a set of relatively fixed *beliefs*. Our beliefs guide us in handling the world that we image. Let's call our beliefs R – 1, one part of the rational circle; call our images R – 2, the second element in our rational capacity.

Thus, beliefs and images are two operations of the rational circle. As fallen image-bearers we are determined to find satisfaction for our longings without ever acknowledging the authority of God and approaching him on his terms. So we interpret our worlds in a fashion that encourages and nurtures our commitment to self-reliance. The beliefs and images we develop are not imposed on us by the world. We actively select certain perceptions and ideas (within a range determined by our unique environments) that allow us to continue walking the path of independence. It is precisely these images and beliefs that must be exposed, repented of, and changed.

*A renewed mind involves a shift from images and beliefs that preserve independence to images and beliefs that require dependence.*

To understand better how images and beliefs are chosen by fallen human beings to nourish foolish resolves to succeed without God, we need to consider how these rational operations develop.

### Images

As a child experiences his world, he forms mental pictures of it. A blind child still "sees" his world through other senses. The pictures continue even when the triggering event passes. It is this capacity to represent reality in our minds that allows us to do more than merely respond to present stimulation. We learn to respond not to the world, but to *our pictures* of the world.

Sometimes the pictures register rather strongly, etching a deep imprint on our mental retinas. When experiences penetrate to deep parts within us — namely, our longings for love and value — the pictures of those experiences are not easily forgotten.

If those touching pictures are elicited repeatedly by a consistent sort of experience, the theme of those pictures becomes an *image*, a relatively fixed representation of how things really are. For example, when a child sees her father's angry expression as a regular reaction to her own clumsiness, she may come to image people in authority as always potentially upset and herself as hopelessly inept.

Images of oneself and others can, of course, be more pleasant. A gentle, strong father may generate an image of authority figures as benevolent and worthy of trust and an image of oneself as competent.

Although images may be pleasant or unpleasant, there will always be a core image of ourselves that is profoundly painful. Consider why this must be so.

No parent, cousin, or pastor can ever provide complete satisfaction to a thirsty image-bearer. We were designed for God; no one else will do. Yet all of us turn to mere mortals to find the satisfaction we crave. There is no one who seeks after God.

Therefore every child must at some level view her world as disappointing and herself as disappointed. We are all in pain without the fullness that comes only from God.

Pain is motivating. We want it relieved. If we believe that the reason for our disappointment lies finally in an unkind world, then we are at its mercy — helpless, vulnerable, and unable to depend on our own resources to make things better.

But if the fault is ours, if we are disappointed because of a flaw in us, then there is hope. To image ourselves as unlikable for a particular reason lets us hang on to the deception that perhaps we can maneuver our world into giving us what we want — either by hiding our defect behind a wall of whatever is valued, or by correcting the defect. Now I have something to do, something over which I exercise at least some control. Life is within my grasp.

> We were designed for God; no one else will do.

What must be fiercely avoided is the realization that I am unloved for reasons that I can neither change nor conceal. Nothing puts me in touch with my essential dependence like the terrible reality of my own helplessness to manipulate someone to thoroughly accept me. The fact is that I have no idea whatsoever how to make life really work. I live in a confusion that forces me to admit my dependence.

But it is exactly this admission that fallen human beings refuse to make. To avoid admitting my confusion, I must do better than see myself as disappointed and empty for reasons that I cannot control. And so I select an image of myself that highlights a flaw, something I can work on. The image may be painful (inept, stupid, ugly), but it protects me from a greater pain, the pain of acknowledged helplessness.

Even a painful image of oneself provides a basis for handling life. If I see myself as clumsy and can blame my troubles in life on the curse of ineptitude, then I have a direction in which to move in my pursuit of satisfaction. Perhaps I can scout about to see where I have some skill while I resolutely steer clear of those areas where my awkwardness is most pronounced. Sometimes the social misfit becomes the library scholar.

The point to grasp is this: *We select a painful image of ourselves* (from a range of possibilities that our environments present) *in order to avoid the greater pain of acknowledged helplessness.* Images serve a defensive function in helping us to ignore the threatening reality of confusion by providing us with an order that nourishes the hope that life is available to us through our own maneuvering.

Thus dependence, the route to real life, is avoided; independence, the cherished route to death, is preserved. Images that give us the hope of life through independence need to be changed. The strength behind the image — the determination to find life without God — requires repentance. When the pursuit of life through our own efforts is abandoned, the defensive image loses its hold.

## Beliefs

Our ability to string together words into sentences that express a thought makes it possible for us to determine what specific direction we choose to go in as we look for life. We form *beliefs* about how our worlds work and how we can function in our worlds in order to enjoy the satisfaction our hearts desire.

The child whose awkwardness never fails to provoke Dad to anger has learned to see herself as a clumsy kid in a world where clumsiness is rejected. These perceptions of herself and her world constitute her primary images.

Her task now becomes to figure out a *strategy* by which a clumsy kid in a world that rejects clumsiness can find a measure of happiness. Because she is sinfully committed to independence as the route to life, she must come up with a strategy over which she has full control.

As with images, one's particular environment limits the range of strategies that may be employed. Perhaps this clumsy girl has a mother who is terribly conscious of her social standing. (The example is oversimplified for the sake of illustration). Therefore she may highly value graciousness and courtesy in her children, especially in the presence of socially "important" company.

The girl observes her mother's warm smile whenever she behaves well with other adults, saying things like, "Thank you," and "It's been a pleasure to meet you." So her corrupted rational faculties may arrive at an idea for gaining what she deeply wants. Perhaps sociability could serve as her route to acceptance and value. If she is too clumsy to carry a glass of water without spilling it, maybe she can put people at ease with well-chosen words. A few successful experiences could confirm her mistaken belief that sociability leads to life.

Depending on a host of factors (such as opportunity and natural talents), this child may become a maître d' in a posh restaurant, a prosperous salesperson, a smooth-talking politician, or a well-loved pastor regarded by her congregation as a caring people-person. The motivation energizing her pursuits will likely be labeled (by herself and others) as a love for people coupled with a fortunate ability to relate well. Her ability to win approval through sociability may even be hailed as a spiritual gift.

Beneath her lifestyle, however, is a sinful and foolish belief: sociability is the route to life. Real change from an unhealthy person who lives for herself to a healthy person who loves and lives for God requires a change in that belief. It must be identified and exposed for what it is — part of a commitment to make life work without God. Her confident belief in herself amounts to rebellious unbelief in God. The only cure is repentance.

Images and beliefs — capacities of the rational circle employed by fallen people to maintain the illusion that we do not need God. We love to think that there is no confusion that renders us helpless; we prefer to explain our unhappiness in terms of flaws that we can conceal or correct. We are not impotent, says proud humankind; there are things we can do that we believe will lead to life. Satan promises life if we take matters into our own hands. God promises life if we admit our sinfulness, accept Christ as Savior, and face the hopeless confusion of life without Christ. A renewed mind involves abandoning the images that protect us from that confusion and changing our minds about the route to real life.

## Victims or Agents?

In counseling, it is often helpful to explore the client's background to understand better the influences that shaped his defensive images and beliefs. Such exploration may clarify the specific content of a person's images and beliefs. As soon as the notion of looking into the past is mentioned, many Christians immediately suspect (with good reason) that responsibility for a person's present behavior will be shifted from that person to his parents. People may then be treated as helpless victims who need understanding and liberation from the shackles of the past rather than as responsible agents who need exhortation to take hold of their lives in a mature, godly fashion.

Because images and beliefs take initial shape through the inevitable disappointments of childhood, identifying the specifics of those disappointments will often help people more clearly recognize the images and beliefs by which they govern their lives. As the past is discussed, counselors must openly admit that we are *victims* of our parents. The girl who was molested at age ten is a victim of her sinful, perverse father. Each of us is a victim of imperfect parents, some of course much worse than others.

But more importantly, we are also *agents*, responsible image-bearers who stubbornly refuse to turn to God for the life we fail to find in our parents. The images we form are not simply the necessary imprint of the parental treatment we received; they are rather *chosen* to provide us with a basis for handling our world with our own resources. The beliefs we accept are more than a reflection of the ideas we were taught; they are carefully crafted efforts to lay out a strategy for minimizing pain and gaining whatever satisfaction can be found.

Transformation depends on renewing our minds, not on changing our circumstances, past or present. Healing the memory of past trauma or rearranging our current situation fails to address the real problem. The struggles we experience have more to do with the defensive images and beliefs we hold *right now* than with the manner in which our parents victimized us. And because those images and beliefs are part of our pursuit of life apart from God, the remedy centrally involves repentance of the foolish idea that life exists apart from God and redirection to handle life according to God's instructions.

Understanding where we have been victimized provides us with rich opportunity to practice forgiveness. Understanding how we have chosen to respond to what has happened to us defines where we need to repent.

Let me summarize this chapter.

1.  We are not only personal beings who long for what this
    world without God can never provide, but also rational
    beings who form ideas about who we are and how we can
    find the fullness we desire.
2.  As rational beings we develop images of ourselves and the
    world that represent our chosen understanding of how
    things really are, and we formulate beliefs that, among other
    things, guide us in our search for relationship and impact.
3.  Because we are fallen, our wisdom has degenerated into
    foolishness. We use our thinking capacities to maintain
    the fiction that life can work without God.

    a.  The images we tenaciously cling to are chosen to
        help us avoid the reality of confusion and helpless-
        ness, a reality that would require us to face what we
        are determined most to avoid — the need for vulner-
        able trust. To put it differently, our images of our-
        selves and our world reduce confusion and therefore
        permit the illusion of independence to continue.

    b.  Beliefs are developed within the framework of our
        understanding of things (that is, images). The central
        ones involve convictions about how people like us
        can find satisfaction in the world as we perceive it.
        Beliefs about the route to satisfaction suggest direc-
        tions to pursue and thus nourish illegitimate hope.

4.  Living in dependence on what other people can provide
    leads to profound disappointment. The emptiness is pain-
    ful. If the reality of that disappointment were honestly
    faced, our commitment to making it without God would
    be weakened and eventually abandoned. But fallen human
    beings are stubborn; our dreams of independence do not
    die easily. In order to keep alive our foolish dreams, the
    reality of personal emptiness must to some degree be

disowned. We therefore deny the intensity of our pain and minimize the disappointment of moving toward people and finding nothing that deeply satisfies. We selectively ignore those parts of reality that expose the foolishness of our commitment to independence.

5. The final defense against facing our disappointment and impotence takes place in the rational circle. We hold on to (a) images that "explain" our disappointment ("I'm really just an ugly, pimple-faced kid — no wonder people don't like me") and (b) beliefs that pump us with the hope that things could be different if only ... ("If I could just find something I do really well, then life would be satisfying").

6. Until we deal with the sinfulness of our commitment to independence and our foolish pursuit of false hope (which is idolatry), we are not touching the real problem within the human personality. Change toward godliness requires a return to dependence. Images and beliefs that preserve independence must therefore be identified and abandoned.

Two topics remain to complete our discussion of the rational circle, and these are the focus of the next chapter:

- Are we conscious of all that needs to be dealt with, or have important motives for behaving been buried in an "unconscious" part of our minds? Is the unconscious a biblical concept?

- If the root problem behind all surface problems is sin, then repentance must be centrally involved in all meaningful change. Because repentance has so often been trivialized by associating it with apologizing for behavioral error, a richer view is called for. If sin is understood to include more than the visible part of the iceberg, then a deeper understanding of repentance must be developed that deals with the hidden sins of the heart.

## Chapter 9

# The Beginning of Change: Repentance

## The Unconscious

When psychologists refer to the idea of an unconscious, many evangelicals quickly assume that secular training is having a stronger influence on their thinking than the teachings of Scripture. Because Freud was the first to systematize and emphasize how unconscious forces affect behavior, it is commonly accepted that the idea is more psychiatric than theological. As a result, while the church exhorts people to do what they consciously know to do, psychotherapists deal with the casualties of the church, people who sense that mysterious forces within are frustrating their efforts to obey.

There is, however, a growing movement in Christian churches that has resurrected the idea of an unconscious, but with significant changes from Freud's view. Another gospel has found its way into the church. The "good news" is that trust in the goodness of God reliably brings about the blessings we need to enjoy the good life. According to this gospel, the unconscious must not be regarded as a repository of *dangerous urges* needing to be understood and harnessed. The emphasis is rather on the *hidden potential* of the human personality, a reservoir of creative capacities of which we are largely unaware. "Releasing the unconscious" amounts to getting in touch with the power that releases God to provide the blessings we think we need to restore our joy.

The unconscious, in my view, is neither a derivative of secular Freudian thinking smuggled into Christian theology nor a thrilling but untapped resource with which I can manipulate God to get what I want. My understanding of unconscious elements within the personality is rooted in the biblical teaching that, above all else, our hearts are deceitful and desperately wicked.

In Hebrews 3:13 we are told to deal regularly with each other in a way that interferes with a process that is natural to fallen humanity — the hardening that results from the deceitfulness of sin. Apparently it is possible, even normal, to be so deceived about our sinfulness that we become stubbornly unaware of internal corruption.

Think again about the metaphor of an iceberg. Above the waterline are conscious behaviors, beliefs, and emotions. Below the waterline is a network of images and beliefs that we choose to hold but that we refuse to identify clearly. We direct our lives according to a set of ideas of which we remain largely unaware (fig. 9.1).

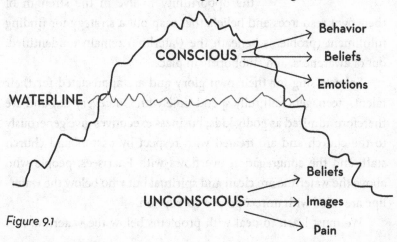

Figure 9.1

159

Too often, evangelical seminaries equip their students to minister only above the waterline:

- To exegete the Scripture and proclaim truth, teaching people what to believe;
- To exhort people to behave consistently with God's instructions;
- To encourage people to persevere in obedience regardless of the emotions that they feel.

Each of these tasks is legitimate, vital, and right. *But if no work is done beneath the waterline, then work above the waterline results in a disastrous externalism in which visible conformity to local standards is all that matters.* That community will be characterized by pressure, judgmentalism, legalism, and pride rather than by deep love for God and for others.

> Pastors and other Christian leaders who work only above the waterline produce either robots or rebels.

Pastors and other Christian leaders who work only above the waterline produce either robots or rebels. And the robots, who agreeably conform to expectations, continue in their unconscious pursuit of broken cisterns that can hold no water. Images that preserve the opportunity to live in the strength of their own resources and beliefs that map out a strategy for finding fulfillment (problems beneath the waterline) remain unidentified, out of awareness, and stubbornly in place.

Soloists sing for their own glory and are appreciated for their talents; teenagers faithfully spend time with God every day and are therefore admired as godly kids; business executives give generously to the church and are treated with respect by pastors and church staff; and the congregation overflows with Pharisees, people who above the waterline are clean and spiritual but who below the waterline are filled with unrecognized corruption.

We must learn to deal with problems below the waterline that typically remain unidentified but still have serious effects on how we live. We must understand what is going on within the personality and figure out how to help people deal with those parts that block movement toward increasing dependence on God.

Some Christians affirm the importance of unconscious content but then wrap everything below the waterline into a single package and present it to the Holy Spirit for treatment. They thereby avoid responsibility for facing the painful reality of confusion and helplessness and actively countering defensive images and beliefs through choosing the path of dependence. Healing prayer, spiritual disciplines, and blessings theology often share a common theme: facing wrong directions that are painful to realize and repenting of them is no longer at the exact center of the change process. It is no longer *minds* that need renewal; it is rather some internal psychological condition for which we bear no responsibility (we are victims), which must be changed by a mystical operation of the Spirit. Active repentance is replaced by passive yielding.

There are, I believe, processes going on within our personalities that determine the directions we move, the strategies we use to protect ourselves from personal circle pain and to pursue anticipated pleasure. Once these processes are acknowledged, there is a strong but dangerous tendency to invest these processes with an identity of their own. The battle is now waged between "me" and "it." I struggle with an internal agent (almost another person), which fights me for control.[1] When I do something wrong, a *force other than I* gets the blame. An appropriate sense of personal responsibility is thereby weakened. The usual psychoanalytic idea is that these processes somehow control me. I become a victim of forces within me that are not me.

Freud referred to the conscious self as "I" — *das Ich*. Significantly, he called the unconscious part of one's personality "it" — *das Es*. The effect of this thinking is to divide the human personality into a part for which I am responsible and a part for which I am not responsible.

161

It is true that we are all both victims and agents. *But I do not believe that we are victims of our unconscious.* We are, of course, victims of what others do to us. Yet the images and beliefs that we develop in the context of our environment represent our *chosen efforts* to make sense of our worlds in a way that maintains our independence.

Within ourselves, we are entirely agents. We culpably choose to formulate images that shield us from the confusion that terrorizes our independent souls, and we culpably choose to hold beliefs that offer the promise of satisfaction without God.

To affirm the existence of unconscious realities within people in no way requires that we compromise the biblical insistence on human responsibility. There is no need to hang on to the concept of responsibility by denying unconscious realities within people.

There is an unconscious. We are simply not aware of all that we are doing in our deceitful hearts. And we *don't want* to be aware of what we really believe and the direction we in fact are moving. We *don't want* to feel the relational pain that threatens to destroy us. But our pain, and the strategies we use to run from pain, must be faced. Pain can drive us to the Lord. Wrong strategies should be met with repentance and redirection.

Because of our commitment to remain in control of our world for purposes of self-protection, we are unwilling to experience our desperate pain and to repent of our sinful strategies. *It is therefore true people do not see themselves clearly until they are exposed by another.*

God has provided three instruments to promote self-exposure:

- The Word of God (Hebrews 4:12 – 13)
- The Spirit of God (Psalm 139:23 – 24)
- The People of God (Hebrews 3:13)

It is my responsibility to solicit help actively from these three agencies to understand better the wrong directions I am unconsciously choosing and to cooperate with them as they seek to expose me.

## Contents of the Unconscious

What precisely needs to be exposed? What is happening within me that I am stubbornly committed never to face? What parts of me are unconscious? I suggest that two major elements are unconscious and require exposure: (1) relational pain, and (2) self-protective patterns of relating.

### Relational Pain

Depending on others for the deep satisfaction that only God can provide is painful. Because none of us naturally or perfectly pursues God as the satisfier of the soul, each of us is in some kind of pain. We ache with emptiness and tremble in our vulnerability.

But many people would report that at worst they feel a bit lonely, or on occasion perhaps more deeply sad. Most of us are more aware of anger and greed and selfishness than of profound hurt. Why? If a core emptiness throbs in the heart of every person who imperfectly trusts the Lord for fullness, why do so many not feel it?

Image-bearers can handle their longings in only one of two ways: Either we can turn to God and cling with stubborn intensity to him when life threatens to rip out our very souls, or we can deny the depth and meaning of our pain and keep on working to feel better without sacrificing our independence. None of us perfectly elects the first choice and most don't even consider it.

The point to notice is that in order to preserve our commitment to self-sufficiency, the unbearable intensity of life's disappointments must be minimized. And life's greatest disappointments occur in our closest relationships. Where we depend and demand the most, we most acutely feel the disappointment of unrealized hopes. Because we choose to underplay the fullness of our hurt, relational pain exists unrecognized. We become unconscious of it.

### Relational Strategies

But still the pain exists, and we are motivated to find relief. As relational beings we devise strategies for responding to life that will keep the pain out of awareness and, we hope, gain at least a measure of the satisfaction we want. The particular strategies we develop emerge as the product of our images of ourselves and the world and our beliefs about what can be done.

Our strategies essentially consist of interpersonal styles of relating that help us to achieve what we want: a level of *distance* from others that ensures invulnerability to further hurt, and a level of *contact* that allows others to touch us in ways that feel good. The balance is difficult to maintain: close enough to be affirmed, but far enough away to run little risk of serious hurt.

Some people are warmly acquiescing in their efforts to avoid conflict graciously. I asked one seminar participant who asked for time to chat what he would do if I rudely said, "No, I don't feel like talking to you. Take off!" He smiled and said, "I guess I'd feel a bit miffed, but I'd thank you and walk away." Others would respond quite differently. Some might be brusquely assertive and seem to welcome conflict. Still others present themselves as quiet, wise, and strong.

Although natural differences account for much of our interpersonal style, beneath every method of relating can be found a commitment to self-interest, a determination to protect oneself from more relational pain. Yet most of us are not aware of the self-protective motivations beneath our social strategies. Why not?

> Part of the self-deception we practice is the denial of what our motives really are to the point where we simply do not see them.

In Proverbs 20:5 the purposes of a person's heart are said to be like deep waters. In shallow water you can see bottom. In deep water you can't. Part of the self-deception we practice is the denial of what our motives really are to the point where we simply do not see them.

Not only the motives but also the unique theme or style of our interactions remains unidentified. We may see ourselves as quiet or aggressive or kind, but rarely do we see exactly how we interact with others and the purpose beneath the specific behavior. And it is to our advantage as independent people that we keep our perception dull. When the interpersonal style with its true motivation is admitted, it is unarguably manipulative, self-protective, and unloving. And worse, acknowledging our intent to shield ourselves from more pain brings the pain already there dangerously near the surface of our awareness.

Therefore the sinfully wrong strategies by which we manipulate people with our well-being in mind are intentionally hidden from view. They take their place in the unconscious.

Counseling that aims to promote maturity by encouraging people to give up their independence and to trust the Lord must concern itself with whatever elements in the mind are nourishing the commitment to independence. We must expose the pain whose very existence testifies to the ineffectiveness of our foolish strategies for relieving it. Then biblical counselors will do more than instruct and persuade; they will also expose and probe. They will look for (1) denied relational pain arising from disappointed longings, and (2) subtle and unrecognized wrong strategies designed to protect from further pain.

If hiding these two elements helps us to maintain our commitment to independence, and if movement toward health requires the vulnerability of dependence, then we must bring them both to the surface and deal with them. But how? What are we to do with felt hurt and admitted strategies? The answer requires us to think carefully about repentance.

## Repentance

If a failure to enjoy God as the satisfier of deep longings lies beneath every form of personal distress, and if sin is at the root of every obstacle to enjoying God, then repentance, a turning from sin, should be central to our understanding of how change comes about.

Our Lord's atoning death satisfied the necessary claims of a holy God against our sin. By faith in Christ we are forgiven for our sins and brought into a relationship of intimacy with a loving God and a fellowship of purpose with a sovereign God. We then can live as we were designed to live, with relationship and impact.

Entrance into that relationship requires repentance, a complete turnabout in our thinking. We must scrap the foolish idea that life is available on our own and with humble contrition embrace the life Christ offers.

Just as entering *relationship* with Christ can never happen without repentance, so *improving* that relationship demands ongoing repentance. Sin continues to be our problem — a conquered and forgiven enemy, but still an active one. We sense within ourselves a tendency toward self-sufficiency that is not easily shaken.

A civil war unknown before conversion breaks out afterward: the flesh and the Spirit do battle. Flesh (human beings living according to their own ideas about how to find life) stands in absolute contrast to spirit (human beings entirely dependent on God for life). The work of repentance is (1) to identify those interactions with life in which protection from personal pain is a higher priority than obedience to God, and (2) to replace self-protective manipulation with vulnerable obedience.

Repentance involves much harder work than apologizing for losing our temper and promising never to do it again. Sin hidden from view needs to be surgically removed like a tumor. *Relational pain* needs to be exposed in order to understand the protective purpose of *wrong strategies*. The thing that makes the strategies wrong is their purpose. If their purpose is to avoid more relational pain, then an awareness of that pain is needed to recognize their protective function.

A man loses his temper and yells at his wife. He may recognize that his behavior is sinful and sincerely ask forgiveness — an example of meaningful but incomplete repentance. If he opens himself up to experiencing the pain he felt that triggered his outburst, then he is closer to recognizing that beneath his temper is the motive of self-protection: "You won't hurt me again; I'll intimidate you into keeping your distance; I'll hide my hurt beneath anger to prevent you from seeing how vulnerable I am."

Now, with an awareness of his relational pain and protective strategies, he can repent more thoroughly. Feeling the risk involved, he can choose to give up his plan to avoid more pain in favor of a willingness to involve himself more deeply with his wife with her welfare in mind. What he actually does in regard to his wife—whether sharing his hurt, overlooking the trigger to his anger, expressing his anger more responsibly, or moving toward her with increased affection—will depend on which action most completely interferes with his usual patterns of self-protection. The godliness of his behavior can be measured by the degree to which it is aimed at blessing his wife rather than protecting himself. The former is walking in the Spirit; the latter is walking in the flesh.

To truly change, two things must take place: *forgiveness* and *involvement*. We must forgive others for letting us down so profoundly. The value of forgiveness lies in our awareness of what needs to be forgiven. If I heard that you made an unkind comment about me, forgiveness perhaps would not be too difficult. If I discovered that you raped my wife, it would be another matter. Meaningful forgiveness requires full awareness of the extent of the offense.

> To truly change, two things must take place: *forgiveness* and *involvement.*

Therefore it is necessary to enter richly into an awareness of the pain of relational failure before we can forgive deeply those who have failed us. Relational pain must be faced if we are to forgive.

Then there must be involvement with those who have hurt us and those who might hurt us. Our relationships with others must not be characterized by protective retreat and isolation. In obedience to God's command to do good to those who spitefully use us, we must move toward others with no thought of self-protection, governed only by our desire to minister.[2]

Forgiveness and involvement, the two elements in substantial change, are the unmistakable fruit of deep repentance. When I abandon my commitment to self-protection, seeing in it the rebellious pride that is really there, then I am able to forgive those who have interfered with the goal of self-protection and involve myself with those who may hurt me in the future. What I am calling "deep repentance," the kind that can support forgiveness and involvement, requires both the exposure of my pain and my commitment to self-protection and also a decisive willingness to abandon myself to obedient trust.

Many people never deeply repent because they are unwilling to face their pain and self-protection. Some think that when we probe into the core of our unregenerate being, a pleasant surprise awaits us. Rather than uncovering hurt and corruption, they expect to find a new creature who always wants to do good. Releasing the inner person in order to express his or her purity is a method built on misunderstanding.

> Many people never deeply repent because they are unwilling to face their pain and self-protection.

In that view, repentance is reduced to trying to believe something and then letting out a hypothesized good self, rather than yielding a commitment to self-protection and consciously choosing the path of obedience.

At the core of regenerate people is a longing person deeply corrupted with the dream of happiness through independence. At any given moment that person is choosing to live out his or her foolish ideas about independence or, because of repentance and faith, that person is humbly admitting profound dependence and choosing to do whatever God says, regardless of cost.

It is through deep repentance — abandoning manipulative styles of relating in favor of risky involvement with others — that God is enjoyed and people are loved. Forgiveness of those who hurt and movement in whatever direction obedience requires are built on the foundation of repentance. The result is a deeper awareness of Christ's love for us and the value we have in his plan for touching others.

Defensive images of ourselves as clumsy, warped, stupid, or undesirable gradually yield to more accurate images of ourselves as loved children. Wrong beliefs about finding life through manipulative self-protection are crowded out by the wisdom of knowing that obedience is the route to joy. Our rational circles become filled.

And it is repentance that starts the process of filling our rational circles and, eventually, our personal circles. Exposing hidden pain and wrong strategies is the first step. The process continues as the repentant image-bearer does what only an image-bearer can do: volitionally move toward a chosen goal. To understand what movement involves, we now turn to the third element in our definition of a person who bears God's image: the capacity to choose.

## Chapter 10

# Free to Choose:
# People Are Volitional

N one of us likes confusion, because it erodes our sense of competence. We feel better when we know what we're doing and what to expect. Wrapped tightly around the core of our fallen personality is a compulsive demand to be in control. To satisfy that demand, we must live in a predictable, understandable world. If I know how things work and what leads to what, then it is realistic to hope that I can make my dreams — at least a few of them — come true.

Confusion presents a serious challenge to our lust for control. Complexity that I cannot organize into manageable categories robs me of the opportunity to take charge with confidence.

When my car breaks down on a deserted stretch of highway, I feel uncomfortable and threatened. The lack of ease is related in part, of course, to the real prospect of physical inconvenience and possible danger.

But more is involved. I know that I am not in control of something that matters to me. When my destiny is out of my hands even for a few moments, something deep is disturbed.

The variety of wires, belts, and bolts beneath the hood is a jumble I simply cannot figure out. I know there is a pattern to all that is there, but I can't see it. It makes sense to someone, but not to me. And without that someone with me as I stare at the engine, I feel little, stupid, and incompetent — entirely out of control. I don't like the feeling.

Confusion is an enemy to people who want to be in control. Fallen human beings, committed to handling life on their own, must overcome or sidestep confusion if they are to hang on to their sense of mastery. Think of all the books and seminars that promise to spell out exactly what needs to be done to make your church grow or to give you financial peace of mind or to build your family into a happy group of effective people. The considerable appeal of such promises is not entirely to our noble side.

When we are confronted with confusion that cannot be denied, there are only two options for dealing with it: (1) rely for help on someone who is not confused, or (2) replace confusion with understanding.

The first option cuts across the grain of our refusal to admit dependency, especially when the one to whom we turn tells us that his assistance is indispensable. That makes us feel weak. (We may even try gamesmanship in order to remain somehow in control of the expert we consult, for we are afraid of real trust.)

Some people appear to handle this task quite well. We all have friends who can speak confidently and at length about any topic that arises. Neither contradictory facts nor obvious expertise in someone else seems capable of shattering or even bruising their confidence.

Most of us, however, are simply too realistic to assume we know all that needs to be known. As we go about the ordinary business of living, we often encounter situations that confuse us.

- Should I let my children visit that website? Should I make them spend more time reading? I think my daughter may be sleeping with her boyfriend — do I ask her? Am I with my kids enough? Do I buy them too much? Or too little?

- Is a job switch a good idea — or a cop-out? Is God leading me to change careers? Which type of insurance policy should I buy? Can we afford a vacation this year? My wife thinks not — am I to listen to her counsel, or do what I decide?
- How do I deal with my strong sexual attraction for our assistant pastor? Should I talk to him? Do I confess it to my husband? Will my children struggle with sexual problems because of my difficulty — is that a form of God's chastisement? Why do I feel so disinterested in sex with my husband? He's such a nice guy. Perhaps I need counseling. But who should I see?
- Do I just force myself to keep on going even though I feel depressed? Why don't I enjoy things like I used to? Why do I cry so much — over nothing? Why do compliments irritate me? Should I use antidepressant medication? Isn't trusting God supposed to be enough? But how do I do that?

Decisions are required of us every day that expose our uncertainty. Biblical principles provide clear instructions about some things (e.g., do *not* have an affair with the assistant pastor); but in most matters, they lay down only broad boundaries that seem too general to give us the specific guidance we want. The truth is, we spend our lives making decisions, some terribly important ones, in the face of unresolvable confusion. And that makes us uncomfortable. Few people tolerate ambiguity well.

We find unappealing the prospect of trusting God by accepting confusion as a necessary part of life and then moving on decisively amid the confusion. Therefore we feel strong pressure to *reduce* the confusion to the point where it can be ignored. At whatever cost, we *will* regain that feeling of control. We don't like making decisions without knowing the consequences.

Motivated by anger and fear, we then impose an order on our world, the major function of which is to restore the comfortable illusion of ultimate personal control. The final criterion by which we measure the adequacy of our effort to understand things may not be its correspondence with reality. Whether our ideas fit with the way things really are isn't quite the point. We are glad

> We are glad to be right, but we're more concerned to be powerful!

to be right, but we're more concerned about being powerful! The desperate drive to preserve our cherished independence makes us cling to explanations that permit us to maneuver confidently through life. Accuracy is not the issue; apparent effectiveness is.

As a result, our capacity to choose — the focus of this chapter — is distorted into a weapon to resist the admission that we really don't know very much and therefore need help. Better to be assertive than uncertain. The strong, aggressive business executive who is in the office by six thirty every morning, who chairs the board meeting with consummate skill and inspiring confidence, is perhaps further from understanding what it means to be a dependent volitional being than the insecure teenager texting a pretty girl to ask for a date. Our Lord's words, "Apart from me you can do nothing" (John 15:5), may ring truer to the teenager than to the executive.

We want to be in control. It feels good when we sense that we know what we're doing. And it is right to recognize our abilities and to use them with confidence. But our lust for control corrupts our legitimate desire to move skillfully through life, especially when we are trying to understand and learn to handle the human personality.

People are too complex to permit confident and comprehensive explanation. Parents cannot evaluate their rebellious daughter so thoroughly that a clearly right way of handling her emerges. Yet they must respond, anxious that what is done will prove eventually to be right.

Counselors trying to kindle a spark of hope in severely depressed clients know that what they do could have significant consequences, either good or bad. But there is no generally agreed on "expert" approach that they can confidently follow. What they do may be wrong. Only denying the risk eliminates it.

The pressure to move confidently in an ambiguous situation may not only pervert our volitional capacity into an aggressive weapon against confusion, but also create a tendency to settle for premature closure as we think things through. "Good, now I've got it. Yes, I can see clearly what's going on and I know exactly what to do." It feels good to replace confusion with certainty.

Once we figure something out, we do not want to push on with our thinking because we correctly sense that behind our "clear" understanding is a maze of complexity that further reflection will expose. When more thinking threatens to lead toward confusion, settling into a defensively dogmatic position is comfortable.

But there is a price to pay for closing off thought. We end up trivializing reality, accepting explanations that selectively ignore difficult questions and focus on confirming data. We are drawn to precise categories, neat formulas, and carefully outlined theories. They provide us with the comfortable feeling that we can manage.

The tendency to trivialize in order to hold on to the illusion of personal control is evident in most theories of counseling, secular and Christian alike. Psychodynamic theorists tend to reduce the reality of *deep longings* to urges, impulses, and drives. Insight, catharsis, and ego strengthening become the means of dealing with them. If anyone thirsts, let them mature through therapy. Christians sometimes trivialize deep longings by assuming that their satisfaction is immediate and fully experienced the moment they surrender wholly to Christ.

Cognitive therapists sometimes strip the rational capacities of their complexity by listing a specific set of irrational ideas to be challenged through cognitive confrontation and restructuring. Forcefully repeating reasonable sentences to oneself is regarded as an effective means of promoting deep change. Too many pastors "Christianize" that approach by teaching that immersion in Scripture through memorizing, studying, and meditating will do all that needs to be done.

. . .

The third element of personhood — volitionality — is similarly trivialized. In focusing on the capacity of human choice in this chapter, I do not intend to be simplistic and reduce volition to something that fits into a neat package. The handiwork of God will always reflect some of the mystery of its Maker. We fail to do justice to ourselves as image-bearers with the capacity to choose when we speak glibly about volition as nothing more than willpower.

An anorexic girl who won't eat or a bulimic woman who purges after a binge often provokes in us little more than frustration and disgust: "Why doesn't she just eat properly?" The root problem, we confidently assume, is irresponsibility. For the same reason we feel those who consume pornography ought to swear off their computers, homosexuals should date people of the opposite sex, phobics need to face what they fear.

In the face of these attitudes, compassion for the person and intrigue with his or her problems are swallowed up by angry moralism. Shape up, do what's right, live responsibly! — nothing more needs to be said.

My concern with that sort of moralism is *not* with its strong insistence on the doctrine of human responsibility. Psychiatry and psychology have rightly been criticized for sometimes explaining human struggles in a way that weakens personal accountability. That is a wrong direction. Image-bearers are created with the capacity to choose and are therefore entirely responsible for how they live.

The problem does not lie with a tough stand on moral boundaries and personal responsibility. It is based on an incomplete and shallow understanding of what it means to be an image-bearer who is free to choose. There is *more* to be said than "People choose what they do, so hold them responsible" — more, not less.

In dealing with this problem of volitionality, I want to explore the capacity of human choice, to wonder why we so often do not experience what we do as a real choice, and to suggest how a liberating awareness of freedom can be recovered and used to take some tarnish off the image. We can state these concepts as the reality of choice, the loss of felt choice, and the restoration of choice.

## The Reality of Choice

The Scriptures consistently treat people as responsible beings. If a contemporary of Moses picks up sticks on the Sabbath, stone him — he was told not to (Numbers 15:29 – 36). When Ananias and Sapphira lied to their community, God killed them — they had committed an unforced error (Acts 5:1 – 10). The rich young ruler was presented with a choice: sell what you have and follow Jesus, or hang on to what is yours. He made his choice (Matthew 19:16 – 22).

In none of these cases was there any effort to understand subtle factors in their personalities that were somehow more basic than the reality of choice. Many elements may have influenced the decisions they made, but the bottom line was choice. They were responsible for what they did because the final cause of their behavior was personal choice. Any theory of personality that fixes responsibility for what a person does on something other than undetermined choice is, at least in that part, unbiblical.

But more is involved in our capacity to choose than selecting to do certain things. Beneath our chosen behaviors there are reasons for those behaviors that are themselves chosen. We must briefly explore the difficult area of motivation in order to understand how people choose both the *what* and the *why* of their actions.

A biblical view of responsibility requires that we see people as moving in a chosen direction toward a valued end point. If we account for our behavior in terms of prior or present forces that drive us to act as we do, then responsibility is denied in favor of determinism. Our actions become equivalent to the movements of a billiard ball, which can be explained entirely by the impact of an irresistible force.

To avoid the determinism of a cause-and-effect model, people must be regarded as operating on their worlds with a purpose in view. Motivation must be dealt with, not in terms of forces that lead to action, but by an understanding of "personal teleology." The Greek word *teleos* means "end point" or "completion." The central principle underlying my ideas about motivation is easily stated: *every behavior has a goal,* or to put it differently, everything we do has a purpose that we think our actions will achieve.

The volitional capacity in people therefore has two parts: the capacity to choose *behavior* (V – 1), and the capacity to choose *goals* (V – 2). I can decide what I am after (V – 2) and then decide how best to achieve it (V – 1).

A teleological view of motivation has important implications. When I am trying to understand why someone is acting as she does, I ask, "What is she hoping to accomplish?" "What does she want to achieve by that set of behaviors?" Motivation becomes a "here-and-now" phenomena with a look to the future. Traumas from the past may have a bearing on what goals the person values and how she has decided to pursue them, but the energizing cause of behavior is in the present, not in the past.

Think about a young woman who tells a counselor about her shyness. She feels lonely and afraid, wanting to be more involved with people but too scared to take appropriate steps toward friendship. The label "shy" seems fitting: she answers your questions with one word, rarely makes eye contact, and is too stiff to smile easily at a funny comment.

Why is she shy? Her pattern of behavior (V – 1) needs to be explained. *Trait theories* of personality emphasize that her style of relating grows naturally out of her temperament ("She seems to be a little melancholic"). But such explanations do little more than switch labels from a colloquial one ("shy") to a more technical-sounding one ("melancholic"). Understanding has not been advanced.

Counselors with deterministic/drive theories look for causes in the woman's psychological makeup or in her environment (past or present) that require her to act in a shy fashion. Rejection from parents, fear of more rejection, and lack of ego strength may be offered as reasons for her behavior. But that sort of thinking replaces volition with determinism as the final explanation for behavior.

A teleological viewpoint treats the woman as an image-bearer who is choosing both *what* she does and *why* she does it. Her style of relating is interpreted as a *strategy* (V – 1) for reaching a desired *goal* (V – 2).

To understand her choice of behaviors and goals, it may be instructive to look at this woman's parental history. She reported that her father was a noisy person, usually happy, good-natured, and always ready to laugh. As she speaks about him, you sense disappointment and a trace of anger rather than warm appreciation. A few pointed questions generate the information that he rarely interacted at a serious level with anyone. More than anything else, his daughter wanted to have one rich conversation with him in which he would look into her eyes and seek to involve himself with her. But it never happened.

Her longings for rich involvement remained deeply unsatisfied. She felt desperate for her father's meaningful attention and states with passion that she would have done anything to get it. The pain of an empty personal circle strongly motivates people to find relief.

The possibility that there was no reliable means of winning the involvement she so deeply wanted was too frightening to consider. Finding a reason within herself for the lack of relationship with her father allowed her to hang on to the fiction that *the means of avoiding pain was within her control.* She came to see herself as a woman without substance, a person with nothing inside worth a serious

178

response. She had often pictured herself as a nicely dressed but life-less mannequin on display in a store window. Her image of herself (R – 2) provided a framework for thinking through how best to handle life.

Because it was intolerably painful to present something real within her to someone and then be treated lightly, she concluded that the most effective way to avoid pain was to hide from view who she really was (her feelings, opinions, ideas). Let people see only the outside. The inside is not worthy of attention and, after all, many folks do stop to admire an attractively clothed mannequin. Social distance protects from pain: let us call that her defensive belief (R – 1).

With the pain of unmet longings driving her to find relief, and with her images and beliefs guiding her search, the stage is set for a visible direction to emerge as she looks for a way to handle her world. The first element of that direction is a goal.

Beliefs about what brings satisfaction always carry with them a goal to be pursued. When someone reaches an understanding of what must be done to relieve personal circle pain, that understanding quickly translates into a goal. If a thirsty person thinks that water is available in the adjoining room, she makes it her goal to get there.

For the shy woman who believes that hiding is her best hope for minimizing pain, the controlling goal becomes to keep her real self safely out of view. And reaching that goal becomes supremely important, because personal survival is at stake.

With her goal (V – 2) firmly in place, the concern now is to choose an effective means of achieving it. Several options present themselves: a cocksure arrogance might do the job, or perhaps an intellectual style of relating could create the distance she requires. The actual selection of a strategy does not, however, *feel* like a choice. It seems like the only thing to do.

The influence of an outgoing father, a resentment for him that causes her to look with contempt on his style of relating, a fear that she could never compete in his area of strength, and a set of natural tendencies and abilities that limits the range of feasible strategies — all these combine to make shyness a "reasonable" choice.

If someone were to ask her, "Why are you shy?" the thought that she had actually *chosen* to be shy as a self-protective strategy against personal pain would never occur to her. She would be both bewildered and irritated by the suggestion that shyness was a choice. "I don't like being shy. I hate it. Why would I choose something I hate?" she would insist. Yet, when examined closely, her style of relating can be recognized as a chosen effort to reach a chosen goal.

Now a difficult question must be faced: If her behavior really is a choice, why doesn't it feel like one?

## The Loss of Felt Choice

Most Christians readily agree that, in the final analysis, people are responsible for what they do. There is little debate with the notion that responsibility and freedom are linked — you cannot have one without the other. People are responsible because they are free. In most discussions of the sovereignty of God, the reality of human freedom is maintained by an appropriate refusal to put the blame on God (or any other force external to ourselves) for the choices we make.

> Why do our styles of relating to others seem like the necessary expression of a fixed personality instead of a series of free choices?

But when we leave our discussion groups and return to everyday living, the truth that we are responsible people is easily obscured. The thrilling and awesome reality of personal freedom is too often buried beneath the requirements of daily duty and the driving power of internal urges. Most of us, in dozens of areas, experience ourselves not as volitionally free but rather as compulsively trapped. Why? Why do shy people experience their shyness as something they *are* rather than something they *choose*? Why do our styles of relating to others seem like the necessary expression of a fixed personality instead of a series of free choices? Why do some of our repeated actions seem more inevitable than chosen?

I once assigned the students in a seminary class to write a paper dealing with a current struggle in their lives over which they sensed little volitional control. More than half of the men wrote about their problem with frequent masturbation. Most were convinced that what they were doing was wrong, but despite their sincere and intense efforts, they reported that they simply could not stop it.

Counselors typically line up on one of two sides in responding to such a dilemma. Either there is a strong insistence that the issue is not "can or can't" but rather "will or won't," with accompanying exhortations to do whatever it takes to overcome the problem; or there is agreement that something other than volition is the real culprit and a therapeutic search for unconscious causes begins.

What we think about problems with compulsive sin and uncontrollable patterns of response is important. Should we tell a depressed person for whom life has become a burdensome, meaningless ritual of responsibility that he or she needs to take a hold of things? Is shoulder-shaking exhortation to get busy and stop feeling sorry for oneself an approach that takes into account the reality of human beings as image-bearers?

Or is it more enlightened to recognize that there are deep disturbances within the human psyche that can undermine the ability to choose? Just as we would not exhort a paraplegic to walk (unless we fancied ourselves more Christ-like than we should), so perhaps we need to deemphasize the idea of responsibility to someone whose volitional capacity has been weakened in favor of therapeutic investigation of deeper concerns. Which should we do: affirm the reality of choice and confront, or deny choice as the basic issue and understand?

The loss of felt choice is an everyday experience. Much of what we do during the day seems less like a choice and more like something we just do. When the alarm clock unfeelingly tells us to get up, we rarely sense an exhilarating awareness of our freedom to leap from our bed, bound into the shower, and plunge into the day's activities. For most of us, mornings mean a weary effort to get up, get dressed, and get going. We feel pulled along by the pressing reality of scheduled responsibilities.

What causes image-bearers endowed with volitional capacities by their Creator to lose contact with themselves as choice-makers? Why do we preface so many activities with an attitude of "I have to" rather than "I choose to"? Why do we so often say things like "I can't help it" or "I just can't do one more thing" rather than sentences like "It's hard but I choose to go on" or "The urge is strong but the decision is mine whether to yield or not"?

We must state clearly that loss of *felt* choice does not mean loss of *actual* choice. Although people may lose all subjective awareness that what they are doing is a choice, still what they do is what they choose to do. Helping the compulsive masturbator by looking for causes of his behavior that minimize his responsibility for what he does is an approach that violates a biblical view of people. Our efforts to explain loss of felt choice must not deny the reality of choice.

On the other hand, we must do better in dealing with the loss of felt choice than shouting more loudly about the fact of choice. Exhorting an anorexic to eat more usually has no impact at all on her eating patterns, except perhaps to stiffen her determination to eat less. What then is to be done?

The key to dealing with the problem of loss of felt choice is the recognition that every action has a purpose. Beneath every behavior (V – 1), there is a goal (V – 2) toward which the behavior is moving. Both the behavior and the goal are chosen.

But the goal is often unrecognized. "The purposes [goals] of a person's heart are deep waters ..." (Proverbs 20:5). The bottom of the lake is not easily seen when the water is deep. The goals behind our behaviors are difficult to discern, "but one who has insight draws them out."

Let me suggest a principle that makes it clear why wise people would spend time figuring out their goals: *Behavior will feel like a choice to the degree that the goal of the behavior is recognized.*

A corollary follows naturally: *Behavior in pursuit of an unrecognized goal does not feel like a choice.*

The unexamined life is not worth living, and it is also a life in which freedom is not perceived. When I fail to realize the goal behind my behavior, I will fail to see my behavior as a freely chosen action to reach a freely chosen goal. It will feel compulsive, necessary, inevitable.

The shy woman is committed to protecting herself from pain. But that goal has been denied—and for good reason. She is wrong for being committed to self-protection. But abandoning that commitment and trusting God for her very survival is terrifying. A convenient solution is to lose touch with her real purpose; it relieves her of the responsibility to repent of it.

But at the same time this condition robs her of the awareness of volitionality, and when that awareness is lost, a sense of vitality is also lost. Life is experienced as compulsive ritual, a series of responses to pressure and fear, rather than a choice to pursue valuable goals that can be pursued no matter what may happen.

We can now sketch the volitional circle (fig. 10.1).

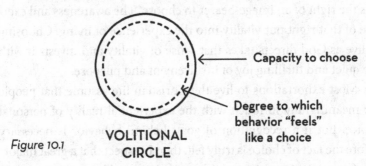

Capacity to choose

Degree to which behavior "feels" like a choice

Figure 10.1

VOLITIONAL CIRCLE

Let the unbroken circle represent our capacity to choose. The dotted circle reflects the degree to which a person is subjectively aware that whatever she does is a choice. A relatively "full" volitional circle means that the choices a person makes *feel* like choices. An "empty" volitional circle indicates that a person feels that what she does is less of a choice and more of a necessary response to pressure. In terms of our illustrations, the compulsive masturbator and the shy woman would be drawn rather empty. They have little awareness of choice.

> When we allow our goals to remain hidden, all that we do in pursuit of those goals is experienced as a compulsive response.

The fullness of one's volitional circle depends on whether the goal behind a given behavior is consciously recognized.[1] When we allow our goals to remain hidden, all that we do in pursuit of those goals is experienced as a compulsive response. Because so much of what we do is aimed toward goals that we never examine, most of us spend our lives feeling controlled and bound. There is no joy in that kind of life. Not only the fact of personal freedom, but a clear awareness that we are free is necessary for the experience of joy. How then do we restore the conscious reality of choice?

## The Restoration of Choice

It is the right of an image-bearer to choose. The awareness and exercise of that right put vitality into the experience of living. Choosing to live as God directs takes that sense of vitality and invests it with the quiet and thrilling joy of involvement and purpose.

Most exhortations to live the Christian life assume that people are meaningfully in touch with the experiential reality of personal choice. But if a recognition of goals behind behavior is necessary before the fact of choice is truly felt, then I suspect that a great majority of people — Christians and non-Christians alike — simply do not see themselves as choosing beings. For most of us, the thrill of choice is sometimes talked about but rarely felt.

We agree that image-bearers choose. And we agree that we should choose to live as God directs. But until people become richly alive to the reality that they really choose what they do, exhortations to follow specific actions only frustrate. Instructions to change do no good when the ones being instructed have no awareness that change is up to them. An important question, therefore, must be asked: How do we recapture the vital awareness that we are volitional?

I recently heard a popular television preacher lead his huge congregation in chanting the words, "I can change, I must change, I will change!" Is that all there is to restoring an awareness of choice? Will repeated reminders that I am a choosing being do the job? Or is getting in touch with the liberating truths of my volitionality a more difficult and gradual process?

After struggling to lay hold of his opportunities to choose strong involvement with a wife who terrified him, a client gave me a poster. The poster read: THE TRUTH SHALL MAKE YOU FREE, BUT FIRST IT WILL MAKE YOU MISERABLE. If restoring an awareness of choice requires that we increasingly face the subtle and often ugly goals beneath our behavior, then the route to knowing the joy of freedom will take us through some painful times of convicting exposure.

More than anything else, recovering the thrill of volitionality requires that we clearly see the self-protective purposes that corrupt nearly every direction we pursue. It is not enough for the masturbator to admit, "Yes, I can see the goal of my behavior. I want immediate pleasure without concern for the moral context of giving pleasure to my spouse." That insight may be true, but it doesn't expose the core of the man's motivation.

Someone who is already fully aware of his ability to choose to refrain from masturbation need not concern himself with "deeper" purposes than easy pleasure. He should simply make choices to abide by his convictions.

But the man who experiences masturbation as a compulsion over which he has no consistent control must look more carefully into his motivation if he is to grasp the reality of his freedom to masturbate or not to masturbate. Drawing out the purposes of his heart (Proverbs 20:5) as he invites God to search him (Psalm 139:23 – 24) and actively opens himself up to having deceitfulness exposed by Christian friends (Hebrews 3:13) will eventually lead him to a profoundly convicting awareness of his commitment to self-protection. Until he recognizes that he is determined to avoid personal circle emptiness and repents of that determination by entering into his pain, he will not experience the thrilling reality of freedom.

The urge to masturbate must be clearly seen as a means of quickly relieving personal circle pain. More than that, the commitment to protect oneself must be recognized as the controlling energy behind a wide variety of behaviors (including masturbation) that together make up a consistent style of relating to life. When his core direction is perceived, the man will be able to understand that the root choice he faces is not whether or not to masturbate, but rather, whether to trust God for personal fullness or to depend on one's own methods for fullness. At that point the choice is recognizable.

When the self-protective goal behind the behavior is exposed and when self-protection is recognized as the exact opposite of trusting God, then the sense of volitionality is gradually restored. Growth in the Christian life depends on a continually expanding awareness of the fundamental choice points with which life is filled. When eating too many sweets becomes a compulsive habit, it is necessary to recognize how ordering a piece of pie is moving toward the goal of protection from personal pain, that in fact we are living according to the lie that *personal life* is available through *physical pleasure*.

When that assumption is exposed, we then have a choice to make: believe it and eat the pie as the route to life, or disbelieve it and refuse the pie as the route to life. When the motivational issues are clearly outlined in our minds, the reality of the choices we face is evident. Restoring the feeling of choice depends on exposing fundamental goals.

When self-protection becomes evident as the motivational theme of life, people come to see that overcoming problems like compulsive masturbation involves a deep shift in *direction* from self-protection to loving involvement. A person's style of relating must be changed; actions that reflect defensive maneuvering must be given up in favor of behaviors designed to express oneself on behalf of others. Changing habits like masturbation in ways that promote both maturity and self-control requires meaningful change in the fundamental goals of one's life. Efforts simply to stop doing the unde-

> Efforts simply to stop doing the undesirable behavior by exercising more willpower typically fail.

sirable behavior by exercising more willpower typically fail. Asking God for help and spending more time in Scripture is part of the answer, but no enduring and worthwhile change takes place without the recognition and repentance of wrong goals.

The process is slow and never-ending. Because our commitment to independence and self-protection is at best only weakened (rather than eliminated) during this life, there will always be more self-protective purposes to face. The waters are deep. But the process of exposure need not be depressing. With every realization of corrupt motivation comes a fuller appreciation of our freedom to choose. And when we exploit our freedom by choosing what is right, the joy of living more closely to our Maker's design quietly grows; the joy ebbs and flows, but over time it takes hold of our core parts more and more firmly. Life becomes an opportunity to truly live — discouraging at times, often wearisome, and occasionally very painful, but in a slowly growing way, quietly thrilling.

The knowledge that, no matter what circumstances come my way, I am free to choose to walk the path of life is the secret of contentment (Philippians 4:9 – 13). Because I know Christ, I can pursue life whether my spouse rejects me, my kids turn out badly, I am passed over for promotion, or an illness robs me of mobility.[2] Therefore I do not need to fear others or what they can do to me, because I am free to pursue the goal that I believe means life: knowing God. Nothing and no one can block me as I pursue that goal — except myself. My freedom cannot be taken from me. To know that I can choose opens the door to the source of all true joy. Restoring an awareness of my volitional capacity through the hard work of self-examination is worth the effort.

## Confusion as the Opportunity to Trust

I should like to make one last point, and it brings this chapter full circle. We began this chapter with a discussion of our natural distaste for confusion. The point was made that we sometimes settle for explanations that reduce complex realities to simple categories so that we can remain confident as we approach life. Confusion is avoided thereby, and the illusion of control preserved.

Now we can say one more thing about confusion. In our efforts to minimize confusion and maintain control; we lose a unique opportunity to experience the joy of volitionality. Confusion and uncertainty, I suggest, are the necessary backdrop for the richest enjoyment of the gift of choice.

God made us in his image. Among other things, that means we have the capacity to move about in our worlds in a fashion determined solely by our ability to choose. A wise person chooses to walk according to God's revealed plan — "trust and obey" — but it is soon discovered that living in this world even with the lamp of Scripture can be terribly confusing. God has not made clear how everything works and what is best to do in every situation.

When we admit the confusion and *actively enter into it* rather than running from it with pat answers, we are sometimes immobilized by indecision. We just don't know what to do. Strong leaders with definitive answers attract scores of followers who fail to recognize that the confusion they feel is necessary and good: necessary because God has not chosen to answer every question we ask, and good because confusion about what to do and how things make sense presents us with an opportunity to draw deeply from our distinctly human capacity to choose.

The boundaries of choice are made clear in the Bible. The specifics of choice depend entirely on us. When we eliminate confusion by accepting glib explanations and following formula-like guidelines for living, our behavior becomes more of a response to what we're told and less of an initiating choice to take hold of our worlds. The thrill of volitional movement is lost.

> The courage to continue when nothing makes sense except for the prospect of knowing God defines a high level of maturity.

For Paul, being "crucified with Christ" (Galatians 2:20) did not mean that the responsibility to choose was taken from him. It meant that his heart was won, that he was determined to know Christ at whatever cost. When life was confusing and discouraging, he recognized his internal freedom to keep moving toward God. The courage to continue when nothing makes sense except for the prospect of knowing God defines a high level of maturity. An awareness of our freedom to move amid confusion and despair makes it possible to reach those heights of mature trust in God. Confusion may be an enemy to fallen people who insist on controlling things, but to the redeemed confusion is the opportunity to enjoy our freedom to choose.

Chapter 11

# Feeling the Impact of Life: People Are Emotional

A friend recently lamented that his life was coming apart. Family, job, church, and health — nothing was going right. When he arrived home after work, he was usually greeted by a sullen teenaged son and a frustrated wife who had "had it up to here with that kid." His job was tension-filled, but financially rewarding — until recently. Due to a major reorganization in the company, his pressures had doubled while his salary was cut nearly in half.

Church life had been a bright spot. But the more involved he became, the more he began to see the petty jealousies hidden behind the scenes. The pastor, an effective preacher who constantly nourished my friend, had just resigned, discouraged by the stubborn complacency of a visionless board. And, to make matters worse, a recent physical checkup uncovered a health problem that required constant monitoring.

Under the weight of these stressful situations, he felt very, very low. The promises of God kept him going, but they provided no relief from the emotional pain that racked his soul. He wanted to feel better, to experience once again a light spirit as he went about his day. But it simply wasn't there. He felt heavy, burdened, unmotivated, tired.

Together we had reflected on the deep longings of his heart. We had worked through his defensive images and dealt with some foolish thinking. I had encouraged repentance of wrong directions that we were able to identify. He had taken steps to change his protective patterns of behavior. We had done limited but good work in his personal, rational, and volitional circles — but still he struggled with emotions that threatened to overwhelm him.

To anyone with the kind of integrity that deeply feels the impact of life, the experience of being swept away by a flood of strong emotions is very real. At times like that, advice to rejoice anyway or to grab hold of responsibilities or to renew weakened commitments seems cruelly insensitive.

Even when painful emotions are less overwhelming but still nagging, the usual remedies of getting busy or going out for a good time don't always work. More "spiritual" solutions such as spending increased time in the Word, longer periods in prayer, or stepped-up involvement in church activities sometimes do little more than push the troubling emotions to a back corner in our awareness — temporarily.

Not a day goes by without some disturbing emotion arising in our stomachs. Whether a trigger is an aggressive person pushing ahead in a checkout line or a bad report from the doctor, life in a fallen world presents almost continuous opportunity to have unpleasant feelings.

In previous chapters we have thought about our capacity to love and enjoy purpose, our capacity to think in pictures and words, and our capacity to set directions and pursue them. Now I want to take a look at our capacity to feel, the final element that defines personhood.

At least three questions must be addressed if we are to gain some understanding of our emotional life.

— What is the source of our emotions? (Where do they come from?)

— What is the usefulness of our emotions? (What can we learn from them?)

— How should we handle our emotions? (What do we do with them?)

Before turning to these questions I want to make a simple but important point that could be obscured in the somewhat technical discussion that follows. The point is this: *It's okay to hurt.*

Life in a fallen world means that pain is inevitable. Think of Joseph, earlier betrayed by his own brothers, becoming overwhelmed with emotion on more than one occasion as he moved toward reconciliation with them in Egypt (Genesis 43:30; 45:1). Or consider Hannah, despised and rejected in her childlessness, grieving before God and pleading for a son (1 Samuel 1:1 – 18). These were godly people who suffered deep emotional pain, and the Bible seems to commend them, not condemn them for it. I want to explain why.

In heaven, nothing will be wrong with anything. But here, something's wrong with everything. A more sensitive awareness of how things should be but are not (an awareness that grows with maturity) only increases the hurt. The stronger our commitment to know the Lord, the more we groan about our disappointing surroundings and imperfect selves. Joy is distinctly an eschatological thing — it is rooted in the future.

Too often we get the impression that spiritual Christians always feel good. A long face becomes a poor advertisement for Christianity, we are told. The hope of what lies ahead is somehow supposed to consume us so much that every present struggle is translated into a glorious opportunity to sing.

The problem with this thinking is that it is *nearly* true. We are to welcome difficulties as friends, to rejoice always, and to rest in God's kind intentions toward us. But joy now is not to *replace* suffering and pain, it is to *support* us through it. Our Lord was a man of sorrows even as he delighted in pursuing his Father's will. He endured much suffering as he focused on the joy ahead.

We must relieve ourselves of the pressure to "feel good" when something legitimately painful happens. Hurting Christians must embrace their pain, not deny it out of guilt. Bereaved people should sorrow. Parents whose children rebel should ache. Men and women whose spouses are self-absorbed and thoughtless should feel disappointed and angry. Children whose parents provide authority without involvement should feel betrayed. Folks who lose jobs should feel distressed. Homosexuals who hate their desires should groan. None of these emotions are necessarily incompatible with maturity. In fact, we shall see later, every emotion can be used to push us on to a deeper awareness of our dependency on God.

> The point is this: *It's okay to hurt.*

So it's okay to hurt. More than that, it's *necessary* to hurt. Hurt is evidence of life, at least as long as we live in a fallen world. Our immediate purpose when we feel troublesome emotions must not be the one that comes naturally: to end the pain. It is better to embrace the emotion by letting ourselves feel it fully and then to evaluate what is to be done. Nothing that I say in this chapter should be construed as justification for figuring out how to escape or even to minimize hurt.

Christians are called upon to face all of reality. Denial has no place in the life of a maturing Christian. I am not, of course, recommending that we seek ways to increase our pain — masochism is a disorder, not a virtue — but I am suggesting that whenever hurt is present, it must be embraced as an opportunity to enter more richly into the reality of a world in need of redemption. The effect of pain can be to increase our thirst for God and our desire to live for him.

Emotions, then, should be felt, not avoided. But they need to be understood. Just to *feel* pain is of little value. Learning to *use* our emotions to expose areas where improvement is needed or where deeper faith must be exercised requires first that we understand where emotions come from.

## The Source of Emotions: Where Do They Come From?

I am sympathetic to the concern of many Christians that we not make issues more difficult than they should be. Psychologists, especially those of the analytical school, have been rightly criticized for complicating the issues of life to the point where scriptural admonitions seem naive. Long-term therapy replaces simple trust. Extensive probing takes the place of relying on God to finish the work he has begun. Life is too complicated, we are told, to think that anything less than psychological wisdom is equal to the task of straightening things out.

In my view, any understanding of emotional problems that puts the church out of the helping business is a wrong understanding. On the other hand, in our commendable effort to keep the church functioning, we must not reduce genuine complexity to simplistic understanding in order to help ignorant men and women feel competent. We must allow as much complexity as the data require, being careful to work within the boundaries of what the Bible says about people. It will do us no good to come up with three-step formulas to explain emotions that fail to address the whole of internal reality.

Simplistic theories that promise quick relief are in no short supply, and neither are the people who look for them.

- Bad behaviors cause bad emotions; so straighten up.
- Bad goals cause bad emotions; so redirect your life.
- Bad thinking causes bad emotions; so think right.
- Bad faith causes bad emotions; so get spiritual.

The strength of the urge to keep things simple partly reflects our abhorrence of confusion. Things we don't understand damage our pride; they put us in touch with our desperate vulnerability—and we don't like that. We want some way to solve our emotional problems that does not require the passionate pursuit of God into absolute dependence. Formulas for understanding and handling our emotions too often provide that way. So we must avoid them.

In our effort to trace emotions to their source, it will be useful to distinguish between two categories of emotions: (1) pleasant-unpleasant emotions, and (2) constructive-destructive emotions.

### Pleasant-Unpleasant Emotions

God has made us as reactive beings. In certain areas we react to our environment in ways that are entirely determined by what happens to us. A slap produces pain, a warm caress feels good. If there is neither pain following the slap nor pleasure from the caress, something is wrong, for our bodies are not reacting to stimulation as they should.

Just as a healthy *body* reacts in predictable fashion to stimuli, so also a healthy *person* reacts to certain sorts of experiences with either pleasant or unpleasant feelings. An act of kindness usually makes us feel good and a malicious deed usually makes us feel bad. It is fair to say that pleasant events usually generate pleasant emotions and unpleasant events generate unpleasant emotions.[1]

### Constructive-Destructive Emotions

Most of us are far more concerned with whether we *like* the way we feel than with the *value* of our feelings. But that concern reflects our short-sightedness. We want our treasures now, not later. A more realistic perspective, one that sees this life as preparatory to the next, tells us that unpleasant constructive emotions are better than pleasant destructive ones. (It goes without saying, of course, that first choice would be emotions that are both pleasant and constructive).

This second category is important and must be thought through. Exactly what makes an emotion constructive or destructive? Constructive or destructive of what? Do we determine whether our feelings are one or the other or, like pleasant and unpleasant feelings, is the choice made for us by what happens?

The place to begin is to recognize that some emotions seem to interfere with what people should do — namely, love God and others — and may on that basis be properly regarded as destructive. Other emotions encourage our loving movement toward God and others and are therefore constructive. They facilitate our functioning in the way our Maker intended.

By this reasoning it follows that destructive emotions can legitimately be labeled as sinful, or at least part of a sinful process within us. Although I believe we must allow that some emotions reflect the operation of sin, there is some danger in calling an emotion sinful. Let me illustrate this risk.

A young married woman who sincerely wanted to follow the Lord was properly taught that certain kinds of anger are sinful. Whenever she felt even the mildest frustration with her husband (a man who could provoke intense rage in the most saintly), she immediately labeled her emotion as sinful and "tried not to feel it." Rather than using her anger to explore more thoroughly what needed to be dealt with in her marriage, she denied that it was there. Emotions must not be denied in fear that some might be sinful; they must be evaluated instead.

> Emotions must not be denied in fear that some might be sinful; they must be evaluated instead.

Feelings, whether pleasant or unpleasant, should be evaluated to determine whether they are constructive or destructive. Once a feeling is acknowledged, the important question to ask is whether that emotion reflects movement away from God or whether it is consistent with movement toward him. If it is clear that how we feel is hindering our loving involvement with God or with someone else, then we must trace the emotion to its root. Something is going on inside us that needs correction.

Whether an emotion is constructive or destructive depends not on what happens to us, but on how we internally respond to whatever happens. Events determine whether we feel pleasant or unpleasant emotions, but *we* determine whether our feelings are constructive or destructive. The presence of destructive emotions indicates that there is a problem within us. Consider carefully the internal processes that lead either to constructive or destructive emotions.

Begin with an unpleasant event: the discovery that your teenaged son is smoking marijuana. The event is unpleasant, therefore your emotion is unpleasant. You feel bad. That unpleasant emotion will become either constructive or destructive depending on the wisdom with which you respond to the event.

If you accurately and deeply believe (R-1) that your deepest longings are in no measure challenged by that event, and if you see yourself (R-2) as a loved and valuable image-bearer regardless of what happens in your life, then the painful event will be perceived as a profound *disappointment,* but not as a *personal threat.* The difference is enormous.

In your disappointment, you will fervently *desire* (but not *demand*) that things change for the better. If the desire is realized (the teen meaningfully dedicates himself to Christ and puts drugs behind him), then the feeling of disappointment is wonderfully changed into *gratitude.* The new pleasant event stimulates pleasurable feelings.

But if the desire is blocked (the boy is arrested for possession of illegal drugs), there will be not only disappointment and deep pain but also *righteous anger.* If the desired end remains uncertain (he seems to be doing better, but the evidence is mixed), the feeling becomes painful but *productive concern.* Options are explored, counsel is sought, fervent prayers are offered.

If at some point the desire seems hopelessly out of reach (perhaps the teen ends his life with an overdose), the disappointment deepens into almost unbearable but still potentially productive *sadness.* Eventually you and your spouse regroup in the strength of who

Christ is and what his purposes are, and you find ways to comfort and help others with similar struggles (a response far more easily discussed than made).

Now begin with the same unpleasant event and trace what develops when the internal response to that event is foolish. Perhaps the father has put his hope for joy in his family (R–1: "I need things to be good in my home if I am to respect myself"). Underlying this belief may be an image that reflects a defensive demand that others come through for him ("I've been mistreated all my life. I'm a weak victim who needs people, especially my family, to understand and be sensitive to me").

With that sort of thinking in the rational circle, the unpleasant event will be perceived as a *threat to personal survival*. The immediate emotion then becomes, not disappointment, but *panic*.

When the core of our being is threatened, the panic we feel strengthens our commitment to self-protection. Responsible action is not the concern; self-preservation is. The motivation to move becomes entirely self-serving. The path to destructive emotions has been entered.

If the *demand* that things change is realized (the teen trusts Christ), the panic softens into *relief* (but with a hint of fear that the problem may recur). If the demand is blocked (your son is caught with more drugs), the feeling of panicky demand becomes *rage*. Parents typically respond at this point in thoroughly unproductive ways that alienate a teenager even more.

If the demanded objective remains uncertain (the teen appears to be doing well, but no one can be quite sure), the panic turns into preoccupying *worry*. If things change in a way that makes it impossible for the demand to be realized (the teen commits suicide), the emotion deepens into an overwhelming sense of angry, guilty *inadequacy*. You as his parents live in sullen despair.

Notice that the same unpleasant event that necessarily generates unpleasant emotions leads to either constructive or destructive emotions *depending on the wisdom* of the internal response to that event. Let me summarize all that I have said with a chart (fig. 11.1).

## The Source of Emotions When Circumstances Are Difficult

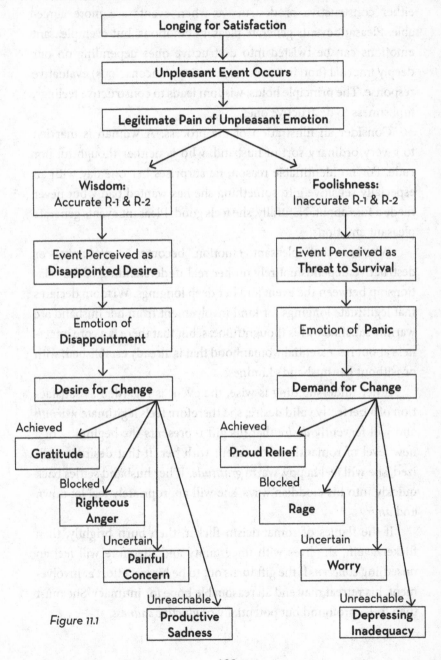

*Figure 11.1*

A similar understanding can be traced in how emotions become either constructive or destructive when events are more agreeable. Pleasant events generate pleasant emotions, but even pleasant emotions can be twisted into destructive ones depending on our deeply internal (and in many cases, entirely unconscious) evaluative response. The principle holds: wisdom leads to constructive feelings, foolishness to destructive ones.

Consider an illustration of the process. A woman is married to a very ordinary sort of husband, who is neither thoughtful nor rude. For no identifiable reason, he surprises her one day with an especially sensitive gift, something she has wanted badly but never made a fuss about. Naturally, she feels good. Pleasant events generate pleasant emotions.

Whether that pleasant emotion becomes constructive or destructive depends entirely on her real understanding of the relationship between the event and her deep longings. Wisdom declares that legitimate longings for kind involvement from her husband are warmly satisfied by his thoughtfulness, but that there is a core intactness about her essential womanhood that is already established, with or without her husband's kindness.

If her understanding is wise, the event is regarded as satisfaction of a perfectly valid desire; she therefore feels legitimate *warmth* and will fervently *desire* that his gift represents the beginning of a new level of romantic involvement with her. If that desire is realized, she will feel happy, warm *gratitude.* If her husband settles back quickly into his cloddish ways, she will appropriately feel let down and *angry.*

If the flames of romanticism flicker, then burn brightly, then flicker again, she lives with uncertainty and therefore will feel an unsettling *concern.* If the gift turns out to be his last effort at involvement, his retreat may end all reasonable hope for intimacy. She must then feel a profound but potentially *productive sadness.*

Suppose the pleasant event of a gift is interpreted through the grid of foolish beliefs and images. Perhaps the woman has operated for years on the premise that she is undesirable and unwanted. Assume that she has defended against the pain of a father's rejection by explaining that rejection, not in terms of her father's lack of love (a painful explanation) but rather in terms of her own unloveliness (a less painful explanation, because it leaves her with some hope of dealing with the problem — she can learn to appear lovely or at least hide her unloveliness). Holding to an image of undesirability (R – 2) creates the possibility that she *can do something* to gain acceptance or avoid pain. She can hew for herself broken cisterns. The basis of self-protection is now in place — she has a premise on which to develop strategies for minimizing hurt in relationships.

Given these internal dynamics, her husband's surprise gift is threatening; she is receiving love for which she has not worked. Unbought love is precisely what she longs for, but at the same time it is terrifying. She cannot make it continue. It depends entirely on someone else.

With an image of herself as undesirable, it is likely that she thinks (R – 1) that concealing her undesirability behind a barricade of good works has some hope of winning the affection she craves. In a desperate effort to regain control of the situation, she may determine to become especially appealing in order to keep the gifts coming. At all cost, vulnerability must be avoided. Control is the key.

Because earned kindness is perceived as essential to her core intactness as a woman, getting more gifts becomes a *demanded goal*. Her survival is at stake. In response to a thoughtful gift, she may therefore feel the uneasy warmth of *insecure appreciation*. Her dependency on continued thoughtfulness from her husband nourishes her commitment to protect herself from the pain of no more gifts. She becomes "extra good," doing whatever might reach him, not to encourage, but to control him.

## The Source of Emotions When Circumstances Are Enjoyable

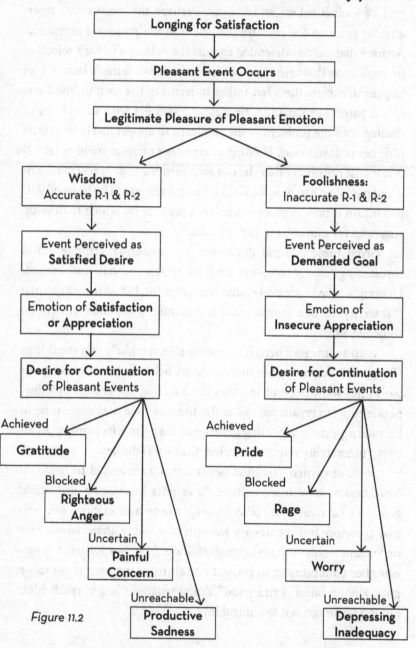

Figure 11.2

If her manipulative efforts are successful (he responds romantically to her candlelight dinner), she feels a pleasant sort of *pride* instead of loving gratitude. She enjoys his romance, but she likes even more the fact that she made it happen. If her efforts are in vain (he blows out the candle, flips on the light, and gulps down the meal), her response will be deep and unbridled *rage*. Perhaps his thoughtfulness continues but with a halfhearted spirit; she will then feel unsure about his love and will sense *pressure* and *anxiety* building up within her.

If weeks with no more gifts stretch into months and even into years, she may grudgingly concede failure. Her best efforts have not been good enough. At that point, her disappointment becomes despair. She will feel *depressingly inadequate* ("I'm just not enough of a woman to win his affection"). With that attitude, she is ripe for an affair ("Perhaps another man could want me"). That is her only hope.

A chart (fig. 11.2) similar to the first one summarizes what I have just described. Pleasant emotions from a pleasant event can become either destructive or constructive depending on the wisdom with which the event is evaluated.

Let me repeat the central point of our discussion so far:

> The *pleasantness* of our emotions depends entirely on the *nature of the events* that take place in our lives; the *constructiveness* of our emotions depends entirely on the *wisdom with which we view the events* in our lives.

A commitment to self-protection rooted in foolish thinking has the power to corrupt every emotion, whether pleasant or unpleasant, and make them all destructive. A commitment to trust the Lord deeply with the core of our being can turn every emotion, even the most painful, into constructive avenues for more fully pursuing God. A simplified chart (fig. 11.3) expresses this central thought.

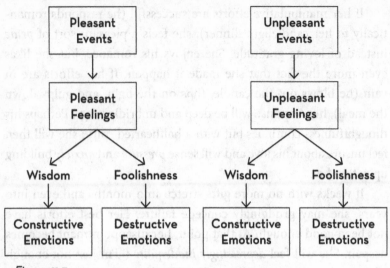

Figure 11.3

## The Usefulness of Emotions:
## What Can We Learn From Them?

With some understanding of the source of emotions, we can now better understand their value. The *pleasantness* of our emotions tells us little more than whether the perceived events in our lives are enjoyable or distressing. The *constructiveness* of our emotions reveals far more. When the way we feel interferes with living in relationship as we should, the evidence is strong that the deep and deceitful processes of the human heart are actively at work, screaming for sanctifying attention.

Emotions then can serve as a warning light telling us to take a look inside or as an indication that we're on track in our efforts to function properly as created image-bearers. It is good news to realize that feelings that rob me of the energy to keep on in my pursuit of God have their source within me. That means I can do something about my emotional problems. I may not be able to manufacture pleasant feelings, but I can learn to mature in a way that will make more of my emotions constructive.

The process of maturing in wisdom is of course precisely that: a process. There is no quick technique for switching off worry and switching on peace. Growth in believing God and seeing life from his perspective is a lifelong process that slowly transforms destructive emotions into constructive ones. The value of emotions is to provide a check on the maturing process.

When I become aware that my internal emotional reality is inconsistent with movement toward relationship, I may assume that I am illegitimately demanding something that I wrongly believe is necessary for my essential well-being. It then becomes time for the difficult work of more self-examination.

The search for the problem, if it is to avoid wrong conclusions and dead-end streets, must be guided by three sources of data: the Spirit of God, the Word of God, and the people of God.

Earnest prayer that God's Spirit search me (Psalm 139:23 – 24) and examine my deceitful heart (which he alone understands — Jeremiah 17:9 – 10) is a necessary beginning. Humble reflection on the Scriptures with confidence in their ability to penetrate my deepest thoughts and purposes (Hebrews 4:12) may bring to light the wrong goals I am pursuing. And vulnerable interaction with God's people may lead to insight and encouragement that can reverse the hardening process of sin (see Hebrews 3:13 and especially chapter 13 of this book). The purpose of self-examination, it must be remembered, must not become lost in self-preoccupation; the point is to uncover hidden pockets of foolishness. Attending to our destructive emotions can lead us to new dimensions of repentance.

> Attending to our destructive emotions can lead us to new dimensions of repentance.

Studying our emotions and their roots is a humbling experience. No one is free from the kinds of emotions that reflect our continuing imperfections. The process of sanctification demands that we not pass over these emotions quickly.

## Handling Our Emotions:
## What Are We to Do With Them?

If emotions can be put to good use in our effort to grow as Christians, then it follows that we should pay attention to them. Because the red light on the dashboard gives us important information about how our car is running, we take notice when it comes on. To disregard it could mean trouble down the road.

Yet Christians sometimes have the idea that paying attention to our emotions is a secular idea springing from the minds of "feel good" psychologists. In many churches the command seems to be *don't feel* problem emotions like fear or jealousy. The effect of such teaching (which is rarely explicit but often strongly implicit) is pretense and denial, an increase in personal problems and shallow relationships, and lost opportunities to grow.

A major problem with the advice not to feel troublesome emotions is that it can be readily followed. To a remarkable extent, human beings have proven themselves capable of effectively denying to themselves that they feel certain emotions, including strong ones like rage and disgust.

I counseled a passive man who was married to a sweet but domineering woman. During a session in which she constantly interrupted him, corrected him, and patronized him, he warmly affirmed his love for her. There was some basis for his warmth: his self-protective commitment to take no responsibility for the family made him appreciative of her insistent willingness to run things.

Nevertheless, he was resentful. Her lack of respect for him coupled with his quiet demand that she give him the respect he longed for generated a bitterness that for years he had denied.

Even the denial was self-protective. To admit to himself how angry he felt might lead to confrontation with his wife. And that was a terrifying prospect, because his self-perceived incompetence (R–2) could be exposed in a showdown with a woman who was too strong for him to handle. That's how weak men think. The successful concealment of his anger from both his wife and himself resulted in chronic, low-grade depression.

Our deceitful hearts are capable of hiding strong emotions (particularly rage) that, if recognized and properly handled, could lead to life-changing repentance. Thus, the first principle for handling emotions is simply to *feel them!* Take time to reflect on what happens, both good and bad, important and trivial. Tune in to the emotional impact of life's events.

> The first principle for handling emotions is simply to *feel them!*

This simple principle has ample illustration in the Bible. When Nehemiah learned that the walls of Jerusalem were in shambles, he found a place to sit and weep. He deliberately let himself feel the emotional weight of what had occurred. The result was a passionate determination to help with the rebuilding.

Our Lord provides further illustration. On the night of his arrest before Calvary, he spent time, both with others and then alone, emotionally facing his impending death (e.g., Luke 22). Rather than denying the horror of what lay ahead through some form of distraction, he entered into the unspeakable agony provoked by the prospect of becoming sin. And through his deeply felt anguish he was strengthened to continue perfectly in his Father's will.

Our tendency is to escape unpleasant feelings with no regard for whether they are constructive or destructive. When a troublesome emotion surfaces in our awareness, we look for a way not to feel it: perhaps a quick prayer or reciting a favorite verse, sometimes physical exercise or a sweet snack or a TV show or a distracting fantasy (sexual ones are often effective).

The point of our effort has nothing to do with pressing on toward maturity; we are trying to be emotionally comfortable. When our efforts are successful and we erase the emotion from awareness, we not only lose the potential profit of self-examination, but also strengthen a disabling fear of who we really are. And more, we weaken our confidence in God and learn to trust him less. The reality of who we are can uniquely drive us to recognize the necessity of God's forgiveness and help. Denying the reality of our emotions robs us of that opportunity.

For many Christians, denial has become a habit. Chronic denial as a means of coping leads to a stiffness and rigidity that may for a time masquerade as emotional stability. People who are neither excitable nor moody can look very spiritual. The evidence of their immaturity is unmistakable, however; people who deny how they really feel typically are unable to enter and touch another person's life deeply. Because they have sealed off deep parts within themselves, they can neither discern nor properly deal with deep parts in others.

Spiritual maturity must not be measured in terms of emotional evenness. By that standard, Paul would be immature, for he experienced highs and lows of real intensity.[2] Although emotions must never control us, they should be felt. Maturity involves the ability to experience our feelings and then either to repent of wrong directions revealed by the feelings or to trust God more fully for the strength to persevere through good or bad times.

In stressing the importance of entering into our feelings, I want to make clear that feeling emotions is not the key to growth; it is merely part of the process. The center of growth is repentance, belief, and obedience. Ahab *felt* his anger when Naboth refused to sell his vineyard (1 Kings 21:4); but he failed to call the emotion destructive and allow it to lead him to a convicting awareness of his selfishness.

> Spiritual maturity must not be measured in terms of emotional evenness.

So far we have discussed the principle that effective handling of our emotions means that first we must feel them. It should also be clear that once acknowledged, *constructive* emotions are cause for rejoicing and strengthened determination to go on; and *destructive* emotions should stimulate self-examination to uncover the foolishness behind them. Repentance and obedience should follow. Therefore our second principle is easily stated: *Evaluate and deal with acknowledged emotions.*

One final question needs an answer. Should we *express* the emotions that we have acknowledged and evaluated? If so, how directly? Is it not right to season our comments with grace? Should angry husbands and wives explode at each other with an undiluted outpouring of what they feel? Or should they say nothing, or perhaps say something but say it nicely?

The principle, I think, is this: We should be willing and unafraid to state exactly how we feel. Spouses who "kindly" share their anger are usually too scared to say what they mean. Their mild expression has little to do with loving concern and is really not kindness at all. More often, they are self-protectively trying to avoid an angry backlash. To abandon self-protection as the route to life means that we are free to say whatever we feel, exactly as we feel it.

*The degree to which we openly express our feelings should be governed, not by fear of reprisal, but by our commitment to loving others.* To honor the Lord as the source of life requires that I voluntarily limit my freedom to say what I feel by a commitment to the well-being of others.

In many cases, I suspect, the effect of limiting emotional expression by love rather than fear will involve more explicit, more direct, and more intense sharing than is usual in polite society. To speak the truth in love includes a far more honest expression of our emotions than we are used to, but it requires us to say nothing that violates the purpose of improved relationship and encouragement.

It may be that much of what passes for Christian graciousness is nothing more than self-protective politeness. Defensiveness, an unwillingness to deal with immediate relational tension, and a failure to listen insightfully to what people are saying are several reliable indicators of a commitment to self-protection.

Should we express how we feel? The principle is be free to express every feeling *but* express only what will advance God's purposes.

Three principles, therefore, suggest a strategy for handling emotions.

1. Fully *experience* your emotions; feel them;
2. *Use* your emotions; evaluate what they reveal about your beliefs and purposes;
3. Be *free* to express every emotion, but *limit* expression by the purposes of love.

## Summary

To complete the four-circle model of personality, let a circle represent our capacity to feel (fig. 11.4). Call it the "emotional circle."

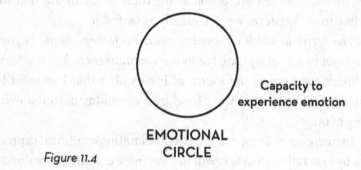

**Capacity to experience emotion**

**EMOTIONAL CIRCLE**

*Figure 11.4*

An empty emotional circle indicates a denial of feelings, not an absence of them. Fullness in the emotional circle means that the person is consciously experiencing whatever emotion has resulted from the interplay of external events and internal processes. A broken inner circle reflects the degree to which emotions are acknowledged (fig. 11.5).

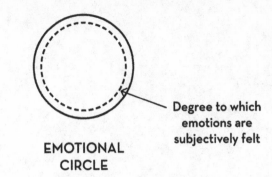

Degree to which
emotions are
subjectively felt

*Figure 11.5*

**EMOTIONAL
CIRCLE**

Emotional maturity is not determined by which emotions are felt, but rather by the integrity with which we let ourselves experience the full range of our emotions. Feeling emotions not only adds richness to life (sometimes a painful richness), but begins the process of self-examination. The emotions we feel are a useful guide to exploring whether we are as committed to God as we want to be. Undetected sinfulness in the way we handle life can be exposed by tracing the background of destructive emotions.

Failure to express our emotions is often caused by a self-protective commitment to avoid rejection and criticism. A *willingness* to express all that a person feels develops as we repent of our self-protection. What we say and how we say it, however, should be determined not primarily by what we feel, but by our purpose to reflect God's love to others.

# Part Three

# GROWING TOWARD MATURITY
## A Restored Image
## and Healed Relationships

Chapter 12

# The Evidence
# of Maturity: Love

I n part 1 of this book, I argued that the Scriptures provide an authoritative and sufficient framework for understanding people. My concern was to avoid dry study that treats the biblical text as a wooden collection of facts to be learned. If we are to counsel biblically in a way that captures the dynamic relevance of Scripture to all our problems, then we must let ourselves be driven by the puzzling data of life into serious thinking and reflection within boundaries that our study of Scripture defines.

Part 2 attempted to sketch a model for understanding people and their problems that emerges from the biblical teaching that we bear the image of God and that we are fallen. I concluded that a biblical model for explaining human behavior will never be embarrassed by the data of human behavior; we should therefore bring to the model honest questions that we are forced to ask as we work with people. Every genuine inquiry should stimulate hard thinking, which will expand, refine, or contradict the model but that always reflects a prior commitment to biblical authority.

In this final section I want to build on the concepts developed so far to sketch a portrait of maturity. In my thinking, maturity (properly defined) is the direction in which all good counseling aims. Relieving symptoms, healing marriages, and repairing the damage of corrupt sexual behavior are all worthy objectives if they emerge from a growth in personal godliness. Godliness (or maturity) is the bottom line. Because it is possible to achieve a great deal of apparent good through counseling without ever touching the essential character of a person, it is important to have some clear ideas about what it means to develop maturity. Thereby we will ensure that our counseling is promoting not only a greater sense of intactness and adjustment, but also movement toward godliness.

> Truly mature people are seductive: they entice us to pursue a God whom they know better than we.

One encounters difficulty in writing on this subject because there are many different understandings of what it means to be mature. Are highly disciplined people whose regular habits lend a certain rigidity to their interpersonal styles mature? Is the warm person who can move with rich encouragement into other people's lives mature? Or does that same person's struggle with lust invalidate any claim to maturity?

Maturity is often defined in terms of knowledge, habits, and skills. People who know the Scriptures, who do what they should and don't do what they shouldn't, and who can effectively serve in Christian activities may be regarded as mature.

But often those who have the trappings of maturity don't seem to draw us to the Lord. We may be impressed, challenged, and stimulated—but not *drawn*. Truly mature people are seductive: they entice us to pursue a God whom they know better than we.

Maturity is less related to perfection than to a growing awareness of imperfection, an awareness that deepens our appreciation of the cross and drives us toward dependency on Christ for anything good to come out of our lives. Mature people wrestle with their sinfulness, mostly in an intensely private battle fought against stains that are visible only to those whose standards are intolerably high and whose awareness of self-deception is disturbingly acute. In the midst of ongoing warfare, they find rest in the reality of abounding grace and perfect love. Mature people are internally comfortable (or at least quiet), but never complacent.

Ask a mature person when she last sinned and she will smile the smile of a broken but healing person. Certain identifiable sins that used to be a struggle may be less of a struggle today, but she is aware of ongoing sinfulness as a reality that corrupts everything she does. Yet concern with "subtle sin" stops short of preoccupation. Mature people know that an unhealthy focus on oneself nourishes the arrogant presumption of self-sufficiency (which is the root of our sin), when it should be starved to death by repentance and turning to God.

But none of this quite *defines* maturity. It gets at it, but fails to pinpoint its essence. Perhaps it cannot be reduced to simple definition any more than a brilliant diamond has but one facet that sparkles. But we must do our best to get a handle on what maturity is. If we fail to define it well, our natural tendency to reduce things to what we can control will lead us back toward an external, tangible definition. Maturity then returns to a mastered body of knowledge, an acceptable set of behaviors, and proficiency in desired activities.

I suspect that a certain serenity emerges from an intimate confidence in God that slowly crowds out self-absorption, pettiness, worry, resentment, and distance, and in their place fills the inner person with the strength of worthy purpose and the joy of satisfying relationship. The sort of serenity that I envision ("a peace that passes understanding") simply cannot coexist — at least not for long — with the ailments that rob people of the sheer thrill of knowing God.

Life consists in knowing God. People who know God are godly.

Maturity is the issue. Counselors must be vitally concerned (in their efforts to relieve depression, straighten out tangled relationships, and promote a healthy enjoyment of life) that they never compromise or neglect growth in godliness. *The task of counseling is identical to the task of the church: promoting maturity.* When the central work of Christianity takes the form of one-on-one conversation about personal problems, we call it "counseling." When one of the two people in dialogue is free of his or her self-protective patterns enough to move insightfully, wisely, and lovingly into the life of the other with the aim of promoting maturity, we can call it "good counseling."

What then is maturity? The Scriptures often speak of fruit springing from our inward reality. In discussing maturity, I want first to think about the fruit of maturity (its necessary visible evidence) and then, in the next chapter, to reflect on the inward reality that makes it possible.

## The Evidence of Maturity

Maturity will be most clearly visible in the way people relate to one another. Bible study habits, ministry involvement, frequency of sharing one's faith, discipline in lifestyle, time spent in prayer, willingness to sacrifice personal comforts, spending patterns — each of these is important, but all can be evident without maturity as their basis.

Just as the essence of what it means to be alive as a human being cannot be known apart from interaction with another, so the core of maturity is fundamentally visible in our relational patterns. God, a relational being within himself, created a world in which separate identities are to function in harmony with one another. The clearest evidence that people are living as intended by God is that we relate in ways that promote harmony between ourselves and others who relate similarly.[1]

A mature pattern of relating involves whatever actions represent the abandonment of self-protection. The defensively pushy person will become more gentle as she matures, while the self-protectively gracious person will assert himself more.

A woman who for years had been lauded for her gracious spirit was committed, beneath the waterline, to avoiding criticism and rejection. Her fellow church members regarded her as a loving, sacrificial friend who always came through when needed. But because her primary motive for service was self-protective, her apparently loving acts suppressed a churning anger directed toward her friends who, in her mind, could destroy her if she failed them.

Abandoning her self-protection meant saying no more often. Repentance required her to admit that life could not be found in the warmth of earned acceptance and to give up those behavior patterns designed to secure her life. The fruit of her repentance irritated committee members who previously could always count on her cooperation. "That's the product of biblical counseling?" one of them complained. "She's become selfish and stubborn."

Though the danger of switching from defensive cooperativeness to an equally defensive assertiveness is real, repenting of her self-protective patterns created the possibility of a richer love. Now she had the freedom to say yes because she cared more about the welfare of others than her own; and she could say no when her priorities before God indicated that the requested activity was second best. She was freer to love God and others.

> The visible evidence of maturity is love.

In a word, the visible evidence of maturity is love. The more I reflect on the love that Paul spoke of in 1 Corinthians 13, the more I am persuaded that few people love. People who love, I suggest, are not always those who look the most loving.

Nice people are not hard to find. Churches, neighborhood parties, and civic clubs are full of friendly people. Gracious people who would never make you the object of unkind jest are known to all of us. Good people, responsible people, kind people, moral people, generous people do exist in tolerable numbers among the other sort. But *loving* people are in short supply.

Love cannot be measured by above-the-waterline activity. Compliments, warm smiles, and affectionate pats never define love. So much of what passes for Christian community represents the well-developed art of graciously distancing one another for purposes of personal comfort.

To love means to come toward another person without self-protection, to esteem others greater than ourselves. Our Lord, as always, is the supreme example. As Philippians 2:7 tells us, he "made himself of no reputation" (KJV), giving up the privileges of deity, in order to experience death for us.

To involve oneself with another for the purpose of ministry is risky. It requires that we concern ourselves with another's welfare rather than our own. Easy words. But vulnerable ministry offered to people who cannot be trusted to respond appreciatively is frightening, and when their response is neglect or rejection, the pain can be unbearable. Continued involvement at that point is the ultimate measure of love. Our Lord died for friends who rejected him and for soldiers who beat him.

Giving up self-protection means to repent of the arrogant idea that life is within our grasp. A client of mine threatened divorce in an effort to pressure her husband into giving her more attention. He calmly responded that to yield to her pressure would not solve the problem. Both were seeking to find and preserve their lives, she by making it her goal to win attention, he by proving his freedom. Both lived on the premise that personal life was within their power to gain and keep.

Fallen human nature is committed to minimizing further damage to our fragile souls by avoiding whatever may hurt and by doing whatever brings the relief of immediate pleasure.

All of us have been victimized by others. Living in a fallen world means to live as a damaged person. It is the commitment to avoid further damage that interferes with our efforts to love. For most of us, love is not the bottom line; self-protection is. But in trying to find our lives through maneuvering our worlds to keep us safe, we lose our ability to relate in ways that would bring us the deep joy of living as we were designed to live. The saying that our Lord repeated more than any other invited people to lose their lives to find them.[2] Yet we foolishly work to save our lives and thus corrupt our love.

The woman who as a child was laughed at for her simple ideas will not share her opinion when her husband asks for it, even though he sincerely desires and respects it. Why? Is it because of the unhealed memory of her father's derisive scorn? Or is it rather because she regards her very life at risk if her husband fails to be thoroughly sensitive? Her silence is not submissive; it is self-protective. Love requires that she voice her thoughts.

Another woman, whose background required her to speak up in order to win the attention she coveted, offers her opinion easily to her husband. To the degree that sharing her ideas represents her effort to keep her husband responsive to her needs, love might insist that she hold her tongue when she senses that her husband is threatened by her words.

*Mature* people are committed both to the abandonment of self-protection and to involvement in whatever fashion will encourage others to move toward God. Mature people are aware that self-protection can be terribly subtle; they never treat the issue as simple (e.g., "Since I really don't care what people think of me, I have no problem with self-protection").

*Mature* wives respond more to the hurt beneath their husbands' ill manners than to their own feelings of rejection. *Mature* husbands recognize their own struggle with inadequacy but do not require their wives to be for them what they want.

*Mature* parents feel keenly the joys and sorrows of their children's ups and downs, but they grant them a separateness that frees them from the responsibility of keeping their parents intact.

*Mature* singles face the necessary emptiness in that part of their souls that only a mate can touch. Yet they still regard themselves as full, open to marriage, and dedicated to ministry.

*Mature* people relate to others without self-protection as their controlling motive. They love. Their actions may be gentle or brusque, silly or serious, traditional or progressive, quiet or noisy, gracious or severe, tolerant or confrontive, but they will be patient, kind, not envious, humble, sensitive, other-centered, slow to anger, quickly forgiving, haters of wrong, lovers of right, protective, trusting, hoping, persevering. They relate to others on the basis of a trust in God to look after their deepest welfare that frees them to direct their energies toward helping others.

> Love really *is* the answer. It is the defining mark of the Christian, the visible measure of maturity.

Something is different about people who love. They convey a *presence* that goes beyond the words they say, the things they do. We know they are for us. In their presence, our growth seems more *appealing* to us than *required* of us. Because the relationship is never at stake, we sense a freedom to enter fully into the enjoyment of relationship rather than to keep the relationship intact.

The visible evidence of maturity is relating in love. As people learn to love, the internal structures that sustain their emotional and psychological ills are eroded. Love really *is* the answer. It is the defining mark of the Christian, the visible measure of maturity.

Consistent with the model developed in part 2, I sometimes define maturity as having our four circles full. Here briefly is what that means:

### *Personal circle fullness:*

A deeply experienced conviction that the core longings of our hearts one day will be fully satisfied by God's presence. With our personal intactness established, we are free to live without fear.

### Rational circle fullness:

Regarding ourselves as entirely unworthy of being loved or used by God, but realizing our dignity as image-bearers by accepting his love and cooperating with his purposes (R – 2).

Believing that life is in Christ and is in no way available through our own or other's resources (R – 1).

### Volitional circle fullness:

With the conviction that life is in Christ, demanding nothing from life but gratefully exploiting the God-given opportunity to love God and others (V – 2).

Behaving in a fashion consistent with the goal of love (V – 1).

### Emotional circle fullness:

Courageously acknowledging all that is felt, with a commitment to be thankful for constructive emotions and to use destructive emotions as a guide to self-examination.

The question remains, how do we develop fullness in our four circles? Or, to rephrase the question, what does it mean to develop the kind of character that enables us to love? The last chapter takes a look at this question.

## Chapter 13

# The Essence of Maturity: Realized Dependency

If love is the evidence of maturity, what is its essence? What defines the character of a mature Christian? People are more than machines that can be programmed to love. They are not just reactors who can be coerced by appropriate pressure to behave as they should. It is not enough to say that love consists of certain kinds of activities and then to exhort people to love by choice.

Something like that is certainly involved. Loving people must summon their volitional powers to act against their feelings on behalf of others. But if that is all they do, if some deeper change does not occur, their love will lack *presence*. The ones they love may feel cared for and looked after, and they may even sense an encouraging warmth developing within them, but they will not be drawn to deeper personal involvement with the Lord. People who are fully there in a relationship stir others with their presence. But there will be no presence without deeply changed character.

As counselees grapple with their anorexias and depressions and parental frustrations, we as counselors must deal with them in a way that creates a greater potential for love. We must concern ourselves not only with the problems they talk about, but also with their underlying character. How do we do that? Exactly what is character?

Every Christian agrees that obedience to the Word of God is central to character development. Although we sometimes differ on what it is that God requires of us, there is clear agreement that Christians must learn to live life as God commands. But character involves more than a commitment to obedience.

It is one thing to proclaim from the pulpit that we must be "anxious for nothing," and it is quite another to know precisely what that means when a teenage daughter is away for a weekend with another girl of questionable reputation. "What are they doing? Should we have let her go? Maybe we're too lenient. But our friends were really strict and their daughter got pregnant. Should we quiz her when she returns or say nothing?"

How does a counselor help those parents? There is really no way of knowing with certainty whether the decision to let her go was right or wrong (unless of course the two girls had been in trouble together before, and the parents were simply too weak to say no). And the decision to interrogate or not when she comes home is not easy. When the Scriptures give no clear instruction to govern specific choices, then the principle is always to *do what is loving*.

But what does that mean? There are no formulas to tell the parents what to do. Their willingness to obey is not the problem. They must figure out what it means for them to love their daughter. And to do that, they must delve into deeper issues within their character.

Loving action is behavior motivated by a desire to promote godliness in another, not to protect oneself. To know what that would mean for this particular couple requires some understanding of their own patterns of self-protection and of their daughter's level of maturity. Wisdom about their daughter and love for her should control what they do.

How is that developed? Seeking to answer that question is where division occurs. Is it necessary to "analyze" and "introspect" about inward realities such as deep longings, defensive images, foolish beliefs, manipulative goals, and destructive emotions in order to know what is loving and right? Does the development of character require personal analysis? Is it productive to plumb the personality, to look beneath the waterline, to enter a realm of seemingly endless complexity and confusion? When we encourage that sort of personal examination, are we not bringing psychology into our helping efforts and deemphasizing spiritual things? Why not just pray about it, do whatever is clear in Scripture, and leave the rest in God's hands?

Perhaps the most common view in conservative circles about how character grows is that our troublesome insides will settle down and straighten out if we fill our minds with enough good teaching and discipline ourselves to live in godly ways. In this view, to ask a depressed man where he felt disappointment as a child represents a concession to psychological wisdom and a compromise with biblical truth. Where he felt disappointed is irrelevant. What he is doing with his life before God is all that matters. Obedient behavior is the source and substance of godly character. Therefore the man must bring his life into conformity with biblical standards. He must be lovingly but firmly exhorted to spend more time in Scripture, to confess and forsake any known sin, to get busy in Christian service, and to live responsibly in the everyday demands of life. Counseling becomes nothing more than particularizing those principles in his life in a context of supportive accountability. That is one view.

Now that approach may bring change. But will it develop the kind of character that frees the man to love with presence and without self-protection? Or will it produce passionless conformity, a lifestyle that satisfies his church community but leaves the man a little less alive and less human?

When tensions develop among church staff, it is more typical of the leadership to do what seems best without careful self-examination of protective defensiveness than to make such examination a priority. The process of looking inward is sloppy, time-consuming, and appears to take the focus away from "dealing with the problem and getting on with the ministry." Nothing requires more selflessness than an honest examination of one's motives in the context of vulnerable relationships. And nothing is more essential to substantial resolution of the staff tensions. The sort of character that makes love a reality will not develop apart from exposure and repentance of self-protective patterns.

> The sort of character that makes love a reality will not develop apart from exposure and repentance of self-protective patterns.

As we attempt to define the sort of character that enables love, I want first to look more closely at our Christian culture's understanding of how character can be developed.

## Two Models for Developing Character

Everyone agrees on the importance of developing character. Parents want their children to develop character, pastors desire that their congregations grow in character, and professors and teachers hope that their students not only learn course content but also acquire stronger character. Although we're not quite sure what character is, we know it is important. But when we are fuzzy about the essential nature of character, we typically settle for producing people who conform to our expectations, and when they do, we attribute their conformity to "good character."

When character is measured by local standards, the model of character development (really a model of sanctification) that we implicitly follow deals only with above-the-waterline realities. Such a model might be called the Acquisition/Performance Model. Make sure that our children, congregations, and students acquire certain knowledge and behave in approved ways. When people know bibli-cal truth to a certain level and practice a lifestyle that visibly reflects the application of that truth to their lives, then we assume that matu-rity is somehow happening and character is developing.

Seminaries too often reflect this model by revolving their curri-cula around the communication of a body of knowledge, the teaching of a set of ministry skills, and the requirements of cooperation with prescribed behavioral codes. Churches do the same when the pulpit becomes central in a community of people who socialize, minister, and pray together but fail to relate openly and deeply about their lives. Families that measure their effectiveness primarily in terms of no visible rebellion and apparent friendliness to one another have bought into the Acquisition/Performance Model.

The key assumption is that *character develops without directly working on the hidden issues below the waterline.* If that assumption is true, then this model is good. If not, then people trained according to this model will tend to become puffed-up, capable conformists who reproduce themselves in their families, churches, and classrooms and thereby weaken God's people. The sinful issues of the deceptive heart are never confronted in an approach that stresses acquisition and performance; as a result, the subtleties of self-protective rela-tional strategies go largely unnoticed. Deep repentance becomes less likely as the crust of denial hardens over the hidden commitment to self-sufficiency.

Similarly, because the deep longings of thirsty souls do not tend to surface when this model is followed, the personalness of our relationship with the Lord remains largely unfelt. Passion never devel-ops. The sort of brokenness that leads to rich encounters with Christ is replaced by efforts to be stronger in the practice of Christian disci-pline. The effect is an academic Christianity that leaves people deeply alone. Knowing God doesn't happen; people merely know about God.

> The ideal soil for character growth is rich community.

A second model emphasizes two ideas: (1) character that enables love develops best when hidden issues of the heart (primarily deep longings and self-protective relational strategies) are directly addressed, and (2) the ideal soil for character growth is rich community. Only in personal interaction can hidden issues of the heart be substantially surfaced and resolved. Call this model "Character Through Community."

This second model includes all the elements emphasized in the first one, but places them in a different context. Learning a body of biblical/theological knowledge is treated as important business (whether in the home, church, or seminary) as is the development of ministry skills and behaving with visible purity.

But none of these areas becomes the core. *The study of people's relational patterns as observed in actual practice* becomes the focus in an effort to identify and promote repentance of self-protective patterns and to drive us to dependency on God, in which we taste his goodness in our deepest parts. Neither repentance nor tasting divine goodness can be as fully encouraged and experienced outside a properly functioning community of Christians as within one.

Character fault is properly defined as a pattern of relating designed to protect oneself from more personal pain. Self-protection is a fault because it reflects a commitment to find life through one's own efforts rather than coming to Jesus for the life he promises (John 7:37 – 38). Self-protective people drink from homemade, leaky wells (Jeremiah 2:13). Because these faults are most clearly visible while people actually relate, this model requires that people meet together for the express purpose of uncovering self-protective sinfulness *as it occurs.*

People who want to grow must commit themselves to providing honest feedback about how others come across to them in an atmosphere of rich support. The feedback then serves as a stimulus for exploring the defensive images and foolish beliefs that underlie specific patterns of self-protection. As the unmet longings beneath the defensive maneuvering are exposed and felt (a terribly painful process), there is opportunity to repent meaningfully of one's commitment to self-protection and to cling to the Lord as our only hope in the midst of unresolved pain.

It is my conviction that the Acquisition/Performance Model leads at best to a love corrupted by unnoticed defensiveness and lacking a presence that draws others to the person of Christ. The Character Through Community Model has the potential to deepen a person's awareness of his or her weakness and dependence in a way that slowly frees that person more and more from self-protective patterns of relating and increases a sense of presence that grows only through intimate communion with the Lord.

In the remainder of this final chapter, I want to look at the essence of godly character. What can redeemed image-bearers become if they pursue the Lord with integrity? How does it happen?

## The Essence of Maturity

The sort of character that makes visible love possible grows when deep longings are exposed that cannot be satisfied by any natural relationship. But such exposure is painful. It breaks us, reducing us to utter dependency. Therefore we run from that experience by burying our longings beneath a host of self-protective devices all designed to help us feel better. In order for the brokenness to occur that can yield a character capable of love, the self-protective strategies must be ruthlessly identified and labeled for exactly what they are: wicked, arrogant declarations of independence from God.

To forsake these strategies puts us in touch with the terrifying pain of vulnerability. At the point of greatest pain, the temptation to relieve that pain by some means is overwhelming and powerful. If, at that point when the urge to rely on self-protective strategies for relief is strongest, we refuse to yield but rather cling to God in dreadful dependency, our character grows.

The richest opportunities for character growth will never occur without experiencing the terrible reality of total dependency. Our natural commitment to denying dependency behind a wall of self-protection must be severely challenged if those opportunities are to occur.

Life in a fallen world is full of opportunities to hurt: loved ones become ill, children treat parents with indifference, ministries are sabotaged by colleagues, jobs are lost, second marriages prove worse than the first, aging reduces the range of pleasurable and meaningful activity. The demand for relief leads to denial of the pain through distraction or compromise. But when that demand is not made, when the clear priority is faithfulness, then relief may or may not come; but character will grow.

Our Lord compared the development of spiritual joy to childbirth: first the pain, then the joy. "Weeping may stay for the night, but rejoicing comes in the morning" (Psalm 30:5). The beginnings of noble character take shape when an image-bearer clings to God in the midst of exposed pain and forsakes self-protective maneuverings. Perseverance in clinging desperately to God without yielding to the urge to protect oneself is the key. It is dying to self in order to live.

Notice that volitional obedience is central. This is no "let-go-let-God" approach in which trust becomes a passive sort of reckoning. Instead it is an understanding of sanctification that deepens our responsibility to obey God and puts obedience squarely in the center of things. The power to obey comes with the awful realization that we are without resources to make life work. Acknowledged and deeply felt dependency on God for life, being utterly shut up to him, is the condition for rich obedience.

Godly character can be defined as confidence in God that one day things will be as they should be. In this present life we groan — something is wrong with everything. But in the life to come, we will feast — nothing will be wrong with anything. Both perseverance and joy emerge from that confidence. With their eyes on a glorious future made possible by the past (Christ's death and resurrection), mature persons persevere with joy in the present. The confidence that defines maturity will grow only (1) when the reality of unfulfilled longings is deeply felt now, and (2) when our utter inability to find satisfaction on our own is painfully admitted.

Maturity — realized dependency, admitted poverty, brokenness: life simply isn't working the way we want it to and we can do nothing to change it. We do not have what it takes to secure for ourselves what we want. Amid acknowledged helplessness and vulnerability, the decision not to blunt the pain through denial or compromise and to repent of any thought that our lives can somehow be restored apart from God's grace is the beginning of rich character. The character that enables love is one that perseveres with joy no matter how painful the present or how dreadful the immediate future.

The effect of dependence on God is freedom to take hold of our worlds and to deal responsibly with them without being controlled by a fear of the pain to which our obedience may lead. The effect of clinging to God is the freedom to love.

It is my prayer that more churches, Bible colleges, and seminaries will intentionally promote true spiritual maturity. In each of these settings, I fear there is too little of the rich community where honest feedback provokes sincere self-examination, where acceptance is extended to people who struggle.

It takes courage to deal with our lives. Transparency ruins our efforts to control self-protectively the images we project. But an honest grappling with life will begin a painful process leading to a deeper knowledge of God. Knowing God is shattering, transforming, crippling, renewing, devastating, strengthening — but knowing God is *life*. Apart from God, life must be distorted to be endured. With God, life can be faced in all its ugliness and potential — and we can become "more than conquerors," a people whose fellowship with Christ enables us to love him and others as we were designed to do.

Conclusion

# Jesus Is Indeed the Way

I recently attended a seminar led by a psychiatrist well-known for pioneering work in short-term psychodynamic therapy.[1] After I watched him counsel on videotape, my thoughts went in several directions.

First, I came away confirmed in my conviction that there are deep processes in our personalities that must be dealt with if real change is to occur. It is wrong to think that disciplined effort to do what is right — and nothing more — will produce the kind of substantive change needed to make us more like Christ. Cognitive approaches as well, whether secular or Christianized, fail to address adequately the important convictions in the soul — convictions energized by passionate longings for intimacy and directed by a stubborn commitment to make life work without God.

Behavioral models for promoting change equally neglect the need for subjective awareness of longings (which is necessary if relationships are to be enjoyed) as well as the importance and complexity of internal redirection. An emphasis on responsibility and visible change is entirely biblical, but not when it diverts attention away from issues in our deceitful hearts that require deep repentance and vulnerable dependency.

One function of Scripture is to expose thoughts and motives

previously unrecognized. And the effect of that exposure is to reduce us to helpless dependency out of which true obedience can develop.

Psychodynamic theories at least make a determined effort to penetrate the interior of the personality. Although their model of people directly competes with a biblical view every bit as much as cognitive or behavioral models, still they encourage an inside look, which is essential to real change.

> When life is exposed for what it really is, the only reasonable options are turning to Christ, suicide, or returning to some level of denial.

Second, I felt sad. World-renowned leaders in the helping professions sometimes deal effectively with concerns that trouble the soul, but they never get to the root of things. They can't. When life is exposed for what it really is, the only reasonable options are turning to Christ, suicide, or returning to some level of denial (which is nothing more than building a house on sand).

Secular therapy at its best lowers the line of denial, thus enabling people to face and come to grips with more of what is true about themselves and others. Just that much makes secular counseling less harmful than so much of what passes for biblical counseling where denial is strengthened by increased moral effort. Moral effort in the midst of faced reality reflects faith; moral effort as a means of numbing painful parts of reality is hypocrisy.

How sad when secularists deal with more of the real world than believers. Only Christians have the resources to live without denial, yet non-Christians often admit more of what is going on in their lives than Christians.

But they always fall short. Without God, two core realities of human existence must in some way be denied; to admit either would require movement toward Christ as the only hope. First is the fact that we were designed to experience a quality of relationship that is not available in this fallen world. In the deepest part of every soul is a hunger that will only be fully satisfied in heaven. The second denied reality is the awful fact of sin. Beneath every nonorganic problem is clear movement away from God and toward self-sufficiency, a direction chosen by the person and instrumental in creating and sustaining all his or her troubles.

Without learning what it means to richly depend on Christ for the life that my soul craves and to repent of sinful movement away from God, all improvement is superficial, no matter how apparently meaningful or satisfying. Symptom relief, renewed energy, and healthier relationships are good only to the degree that they reflect movement toward God. Otherwise, they support the illusion of independence, the illusion that life can work without relating to God on his terms.

I left the psychiatrist's seminar with a third impression. Relationship with Christ really *is* the only answer to life's questions. When I sometimes feel so empty that Christian commitment seems pointless, my mind inevitably turns to Peter's words, "Lord, to whom [else] shall we go? You have the words of eternal life" (John 6:68).

Although Christian leaders too often teach that truth in a way that embarrasses the gospel, still it is true. Secularists sometimes seem to have a corner on honestly facing the disturbing complexity of life while Christians recite clichés that push away real questions of the heart. As a result, nonbelievers often help people with emotional problems more effectively than Christians.

But all their efforts are fatally flawed. Without Christ there is no life, only temporary imitations. And anything that counterfeits life and thus encourages people to press on without turning to God is dangerously wrong.

The core of all helping effort must be Christ. The gospel really is good news. When the internal troubles of people are exposed, when unsatisfied longings are felt in a way that leads to overwhelming pain, when self-centeredness is recognized in every fiber of human motivation, then (and not until then) can the wonder of the gospel be truly appreciated.

People struggling with anorexia, married couples wondering what happened to the warmth, middle-aged adults feeling restless and burned out, young people panicking as they face the demands of life, others hating but yielding to self-destructive sexual urges — to these and to all of us, my message is simply this: *There really are answers.*

Christian counseling can sometimes help. Secular therapy may expose hidden concerns that need attention. Church attendance, prayer, Bible study, and sharing our faith with others should be a part of our lives. Renewed determination to do what is right is essential.

> The answer to all of life's questions lies in relationship with Christ.

But the answer to all of life's questions lies in relationship with Christ, a personally gripping relationship that is entered into in a moment but takes long and difficult years to develop.

My great fear as I write these words is that I will be misunderstood and thought to be saying what I do not mean. Many who proclaim "Christ is the answer" tend to deal with a deeply disturbed person in an offensive and simplistic way that could aggravate the problem. Merely telling a clinically depressed person that Christ can satisfy all the longings of her soul will make as much impact as one vote on a national election: it matters, but so much more is needed to turn the tide. I hate the thought that this book might encourage pastors to counsel agoraphobics or homosexuals or borderline personalities or depressed people merely by exhorting them to "trust Christ and get serious about obedience."

What is wrong with that counsel is that it will rarely be heard. The difficult work of (1) exploring the core longings of the soul through facing relational disappointments and (2) understanding the subtleties of self-protective behavioral patterns as a precondition for repentance must plow up the ground for the seeds of trust and obedience to take root. Counseling and discipleship are not reducible to a five-session program. Helping people to know the Lord in life-changing ways requires a level of involvement with them that is muddled, frustrating, thrilling, draining, enduring.

But the process of informed involvement can lead to the profound realization that Christ really is the answer. In the deepest part of our soul, a region that few ever self-consciously enter, each of us longs for a quality of love that only Christ provides. We long for an awareness of value to another that is available in that relationship and nowhere else. When we enter that hidden part where longings are intensely felt and where our arrogant refusal to trust God is exposed in all its ugliness, then the truth that Christ is life begins to grip us deeply.

The route to maturity is long, bumpy, and uphill. But it can be traveled — and it's worth it. At times the route to life will seem like the route to death. Entering more deeply into our unmet longings and exposing more thoroughly our sinful self-protection is painful. But the awareness of pain enables richer and more courageous trust, and the awareness of sin can lead to more profound levels of repentance and obedience.

There is a route to life. Our Lord is that way. He is the truth that frees us to walk toward him. He is the life that we can taste now and indulge in freely and fully for all eternity. In everything, including counseling, Christ must have the preeminence.

# Strengths and Weaknesses of the Dynamic, Moral, and Relational Models

I t may be helpful to consider each of the three models of humankind (ch. 5) to discern which of the four elements of personhood
(ch. 6) they either affirm or deny. The adequacy of any model for
understanding people can be measured by how effectively each of
the four elements (personal, rational, volitional, and emotional) is
taken into account.

|  | Personal | Rational | Volititional | Emotional |
|---|---|---|---|---|
| **Dynamic** | —┼— | + | —┼— | + |
| **Moral** | — | + | —┼— | — |
| **Relational** | + | — | — | —┼— |

The Dynamic Model emphasizes the deep workings of the
human personality and gives some attention to both thought processes and feelings. It generally gives little emphasis to the role of
responsible choice, sometimes discrediting it altogether.

The Moral Model strongly underlines the importance of choice, insisting that human beings are above all else responsible for their actions. It often gives room for the importance of how people think, but pays little attention to deep longings and to feelings, concerned that an emphasis on emotions tends to provide excuses for irresponsibility ("I couldn't help yelling; I was angry").

The Relational Model focuses most of its attention on how people feel at the moment, sometimes encouraging movement in whatever direction leads to positive feelings about oneself and others. It grants some role to deeper longings, very little to choice, and even less to thinking processes and beliefs. In its extreme form, it says, "If it feels good, do it."

It might be noted that when any of these four qualities of personhood is neglected by an unbalanced view of people, the consequences are significant.

Counselors who give scant attention to deep longings tend to become nonrelational, shallow, and lifelessly aloof and distant. Legalism thrives in such an atmosphere.

When our capacity for thinking is underemphasized, counseling often becomes an impulsive search for whatever works. The blindness of people goes unchallenged, and movement toward God is not developed.

If volitional capacities are ignored, counseling leads to weakened character, where people wait for change to happen to them rather than responsibly taking hold of their worlds as agents of change.

When feelings are cast aside in favor of doing what's right, people become machines who develop little awareness of the richness of their personalities. Feelings can function as a window to deeper parts within. When the window is shut, depth is lost.

# Notes

## Preface

1. It is worth noting that Erich Fromm developed and popularized the notion that only after persons are able to love themselves are they able to love others.

## Chapter 1

1. J. Robertson McQuilkin, *The Behavioral Sciences Under the Authority of Scripture* (Paper read to the Evangelical Theological Society, Jackson, Miss., 30 December 1975).

## Chapter 2

1. John Calvin, *The Institutes of the Christian Religion,* ed. Tony Lane and Hilary Osborne (London: Hodder and Stoughton, 1986), pp. 39 – 40.
2. The works of Jay Adams and Charles Solomon are notable exceptions.
3. No final or closed model of counseling will ever be developed by fallen, finite human beings. The best model will always have ragged edges, which can be partially smoothed out only through openness to new thinking and data.

## Chapter 3

1. The data and theories of psychology may serve a useful function, not only in helping us deal with such things as learning disabilities or medication for psychotics, but also in stimulating us to ask provocative questions about what is going on with people and how to respond more adequately. But — and this must be stressed as the essential difference between positions 1 and 3 — the Bible *alone* is sufficient in providing authoritative answers and categories for thought in determining how life should and can be lived. Position 3 affirms both biblical authority and biblical sufficiency.
2. In part 2 of this book I develop a model for understanding people that supports my contention that all of us, even the most mature, still wrestle with significant concerns that need to be addressed in the context of biblical community.

241

## Chapter 4

1. As I say that Freud refused to look at Scripture, I fear that I may come across as terribly simplistic: "If only Freud had read his Bible, he would have been okay." I believe that psychodynamic theory is both provocative and valuable in recognizing elements in the human personality that many theologians have failed to see. Had Freud read his Bible, I suspect he would not have become a typical, externally oriented Christian. Rather, he might have developed a more accurate understanding of the inside structure of human beings, including an appreciation for sin as humankind's central problem and an appreciation of the deep longings of the soul that yearn for satisfaction. Part 2 of this book develops these ideas more thoroughly.

2. In *Effective Biblical Counseling* I describe three levels of counseling. Level 3 includes what is usually meant by therapy.

3. It might be noted that the further one is removed from direct statements of the biblical text, the more room there is for interpretative error. Exegetical statements — those that affirm the meaning of a particular text — are closer to the actual words of Scripture than theological statements. When we study the *implications* of theological categories, we are still further from the text and must be even more tentative in our formulations.

4. The definition of a "polished life" depends on one's community. In some Christian circles, spiritual maturity is defined in terms of prohibitions against drinking, dancing, or attending movies. In others, the rules permit social drinking but require strict Sabbath-keeping (no tennis on Sundays). In still other circles, loose language, movies, and Sunday tennis are acceptable, but holding convictions that look like narrow-mindedness is out of favor. In every case, the condition of the heart is measured by conformity to external, visible standards.

## Chapter 5

1. Joseph F. Rychlak, *Introduction to Personality and Psychotherapy,* 2nd ed. (Boston: Houghton Mifflin, 1981).

## Chapter 6

1. J. I. Packer, *Knowing God* (Downers Grove, Ill.: InterVarsity, 1973), p. 89.
2. J. Oliver Buswell, *Systematic Theology* (Grand Rapids: Zondervan, 1962), 1:232.
3. Lewis Sperry Chafer, *Systematic Theology* (Grand Rapids: Zondervan, repr. 1981), 2:160.
4. Ibid., pp. 168.
5. Louis Berkhof, *Systematic Theology* (Grand Rapids: Eerdmans, 1978), p. 204.

**Chapter 7**

1. That verse, it should be recalled, was spoken by a man who had denied the ugliness of his sin behind a mask of self-righteousness that God forcefully ripped away. Read 2 Samuel 12:1 – 13.

**Chapter 8**

1. Richard Lovelace, *Dynamics of Spiritual Life* (Downers Grove, Ill.: InterVarsity, 1979), pp. 86 – 89.
2. In our fallen condition, every legitimate longing shares in the corruption. Longings will never be pure until we're in heaven. Our longings drive us in directions that can be illegitimate and sinful. The renewal of which the Scriptures speak does not involve a decrease in the intensity of our legitimate longings, but it will gradually purify our longings so that more and more we long for God.
3. When I talk about images, I am discussing something very different from the imaging recommended by possibility thinkers, positive confessionalists, and primal screamers. These people regard imagination as a tool for unlocking a godlike potential within us to create virtually whatever we desire. Believe it, see it, image it — and it shall be. In my view, fallen image-bearers use their capacity to image in ways that sometimes strengthens their sinful commitment to independence. *Repentance* of these images is called for, not *release.*

**Chapter 9**

1. In Christian circles, the teaching of "two natures" expresses the same idea. There is a "me" (the person I really am in Christ, my new nature, which is perfect) and an "other me" (the person I used to be, my old nature, which is entirely corrupt). A civil war between two powers continually rages within my body. The effect is that the real me becomes a mediator between two warring factions, trying to encourage the good soldier and working to subdue the bad soldier, rather than a single person responsible for choosing the path of dependence or independence at every moment.
2. Forgiving involvement with an abusive husband, I should point out, may mean calling the police and pressing charges. Biblical involvement and masochism are not identical.

**Chapter 10**

1. It should be noted that a loss of felt volitionality may be experienced most keenly in one area of behavior, or it may be a general sense of impotence. And often there is a network of unrecognized goals beneath the felt loss of volitionality.

2. These words come easily. The reality of pressing on when so much of what you cherish is taken from you is not easy. Maturity is accompanied by moments of pain that feel like hell itself. There are no easy answers.

### Chapter 11

1. Two points of complexity might be noted: (1) defining an event as pleasant or unpleasant is not always easy. Perhaps we're on the right track in thinking that events that reflect the character of God and are consistent with his original design are experienced as pleasant. Unpleasant events would thus represent violations of God's character and design; (2) an event, no matter how pleasant it may be, can never generate a purely pleasant emotion. Something is lacking in the best of events. To Christians, pleasant emotions are always mixed with groaning for the better day ahead. Unpleasant events, too, provoke mixed feelings, especially for Christians. In the middle of trouble, the prospect of no more difficulties warms the heart, and the awareness that a good plan is in progress produces a quiet joy beneath the sorrow.

2. I should note that the highs and lows of maturity do not involve either giddy flightiness or disabling depression. Emotions in the mature person are part of a deep stream. Beneath whatever is felt, there is a quiet resolve to continue moving in a godly direction. Strong emotions in the mature person are not allowed to interfere with that movement for long.

### Chapter 12

1. It might be noted that in a fallen world, biblical patterns of relating will often create division, even among fellow Christians, and may therefore appear to be unloving and unbiblical. Although no one functions without some degree of self-protective defensiveness, those with less defensiveness will typically be offensive to those with more.

2. Matthew 10:38 – 39; 16:24 – 25; Mark 8:34 – 35; Luke 9:24; 14:26 – 27; 17:33; John 12:25.

### Conclusion

1. Short-term psychodynamic therapy is a modern variant of orthodox psychoanalytic psychotherapy that emphasizes more active (and sometimes confrontive) interpretative work. Although many versions of this approach are developing, they share in common a concern for careful patient selection, a belief that focused problems can be dealt with in a relatively short time, and a commitment to a psychodynamic view of the human personality.

# Subject Index

245

# Subject Index

Maturity, 78, 111–12, 148, 187, 189, 201, 242n4, 244n2; defined, 189, 192; and emotions, 193, 207–8, 211; false idea, 111, 157; and imperfection, 205, 217

McQuilkin, J. Robertson, 31

Meaning. *See* Impact

Memories, 136, 140, 155, 221

"Message" of God, 70–73, 76, 145; vs. "words," 70–73

Mind, 33–44; renewed, 144–45, 148–50, 154; "right," 133

"Mini-seminaries," 57

Models, 28–32, 38–42, 48, 227–30, 245; basic, 89–90; behavior, 227–228; counseling, 28–32, 38–49, 53, 72, 94–98, 118; character, 225–30; four-circle, 210–11; personhood, 239–40

Moral: core, 107; effort, 210; excellence lost, 89–90; model, 81–82, 84–85, 213; neutrality, 90–91, 93, 99; image, 89, 92–93

Moralism, 62, 142, 175

Motives, motivation, 15, 93, 114, 129, 138–43, 154, 163–65, 185–88, 198, 235; and choice, 176–78; unconscious, 86, 142–43; unrecognized, 93, 185, 225

Need, 9–11, 131; personal, 9–11, 17, 19–22

Nouthetic counseling, 28, 93

Obedience, 18, 35, 40, 51, 87, 110, 123, 136–37, 140–49; centrality of, 225–26, 231; chosen, 160, 208–9; to God, 18, 62, 166–69, 225, 231–37

Obsessive thoughts, 74

Observations, 18, 41, 47, 53, 79, 88, 96, 122, 127

Openness, 16–19, 92

Orthodoxy, cold, 75

Other-centeredness, 113, 222

Outer circle, 131–32

Outer person, 149

Packer, J. I., 101

Pain, internal or emotional, 71–72, 191–91; biblical examples, 179–93; inevitable, 138, 192; minimizing, 155, 179

Painful: consequences, 20; growth, 23; image, 152; process, 118; route, 88

Panic, 9, 33, 198–99, 236

Pant, word study, 119–20

Parents, 20–22, 35, 43, 63, 70, 80, 87, 126, 155, 173, 178, 193, 198; mature, 221–27, 231

Past, influence of, 87, 90, 154–55, 177, 231

Patterns, 36, 57, 60–62, 91, 109; behavior, 140–44; living, 52, 57, 60–62; relating, 92, 109, 163, 196, 218, 229–30, 244n1; self-protection, 163, 167, 191, 218, 225, 229

Paul, joy and struggle, 114

Peace, 20, 23, 111, 171, 205, 217

Peer pressure, 108

People of God. *See* Community: of God's people

Perfection vs. maturity, 216–17

Perls, Fritz, 29

Personal circle, 127–32, 146–48, 169, 178–79, 222–23; pain, 161, 179, 186

Personality: in Bible 142–43; dynamics, 90

Personhood: defined, 101; elements of, 103, 134, 239–40

Pleasure, 78, 86, 127–28, 140, 147–48, 153, 161, 185–86, 195, 202, 220

"Pop psychology," 19

Positive confession, 243n3

"Possibility thinking," 130–31, 152, 243n3

Practical vs. philosophical, 95–96

Pragmatism, 36, 45–46

Prayer, 161, 191, 197, 205

Presence, related to love, 222, 224–27, 230

Pretense, 206; in Christian community, 75, 93, 114, 118; vs. gratitude, 197, 199, 200, 202, 203

Pride, 160, 168, 195, 202, 203

Principles, 73, 79, 86–87, 172, 225; behavior and choice, 86, 183; emotions, 200, 207–10; using Scripture, 56–60, 73, 79–80, 172

Problems, 9–10, 46–47, 149, 187, 215–27; life's, 19–23, 50–64, 75–81; "personal," 136; "real," 9–10, 67, 108, 155–57

Sufficiency of Bible, 8, 10, 31–32, 61–64, 69, 241n1
Suicide, 76, 148–49, 198, 234
Superficiality, 20, 22, 143; of answers, 63
Survival, 120, 179–83, 198–99, 201
Symptoms, 44, 51, 66, 91, 118, 139–40, 216
Tarnished image-bearer, 97–98, 115, 121, 125, 150, 243n3. *See also* Image-bearer
Teenager, 11, 108–9, 160, 173, 190–91, 197–98
*Teleos*, word study, 177
Temptation, 61, 70, 87, 139, 230
Tension, 45, 59–60, 75, 92, 107–9, 209, 226–27
Text, Scripture, 64, 70–76, 79, 103, 215, 242n3
Textbook, Bible as, 10–13, 30, 40–47, 50–64
Theological: issues, 74; vs. psychiatric, 158
Theology, 7–11, 21, 73–74, 80, 87; Lutheran, 102; natural, 34; as practical, 21–22; vs. psychology, 41–45; Reformed, 102; Roman Catholic, 34, 99
Theory, 7–8, 19, 27–33; counseling, 7, 31–32, 41, 45, 81, 96, 98; trait, 177–78
Therapeutic: methods, 20, 136; search, 181
Therapy, 26–33, 91, 157, 174, 194; vs. counseling, 65–69; Gestalt, 93, 136; kinds of, 28; primal, 27, 30, 37, 45, 93, 136; psychodynamic, 137, 233, 244n1; psychotherapy, 28–29, 65, 142, 244n1; rage-reduction, 27, 30; "real," 66; re-parenting, 28, 30, 45; vs. trust, 188
Thirst, 18, 78, 104; of soul, 116, 119–29, 133–34, 193, 228
Threat, personal, 197
Transformation, 148, 155. *See also* Change
Transparency, need for, 232
Trapped feeling, 180
Traumas, 20, 27, 143, 155, 177
Trinity, Godhead, 99, 122–24, 135
Trust, 151, 156–58; commitment to, 183, 186–89, 203; and confusion, 171–72, 188–89; need for, 163, 165, 168, 171–74

Truth, 9–11, 24, 43–45, 72–77, 80–81, 142–49, 226–28; divine, 22; psychological truth, 43; route to, 29, 36, 38; technical, 10; vital, 11
"Two-book" view of revelation, 40–45
"Two natures" teaching, 243n1
Uncertainty, 43–44, 96, 119, 172; inevitable, 43–45; living with, 139, 188, 200
Unconscious: causes, 181; commitment, 119; dispositions, 90–91; motives, 86, 142
Unconscious, the, 158–65
Uncontrollable, 137, 141, 181
Understanding people, 34, 83–91, 106, 215, 241n2; model for, 66, 85, 215, 239
Unexamined life, 56, 183
Unresolved: questions, 56; pain, 230
V–1, 177–78, 182, 223
V–2, 177–79, 182, 223
Value: desire for, 151–53, 237; of forgiveness, 167; of emotions, 169, 193–95, 204–5
Van Til, Cornelius, 12
Victims, 91, 93; vs. agents, 154–55, 161–62
Volitional circle, 183–84, 191, 223
Volitionality, 175–76, 183, 185–88, 243n1
Vulnerability, 92, 115, 139, 163–65, 195, 201, 230–32
Water line of consciousness, metaphor, 143–44, 159–61, 220, 228
Well-being, 107, 118, 120, 132, 165, 205, 209
Wells, leaky, metaphor, 121, 128, 229
Wholeness, 28, 116
Wife, 75, 95, 108–9, 128, 147, 166–67, 185, 190, 206–7
Willing vs. working, 105
Will of God, 144, 193
Willpower, 175, 187
Wisdom, 8, 16, 32, 58–60, 69–72, 76, 113, 147–49, 194–205, 225–26
Word of God, 10, 72–73, 162, 205, 225
Worry, 198–99, 202, 205, 217
Wrong approaches, 89, 136–38

# Scripture Index

# Scripture Index